The
Reference Shelf ®

Graphic Novels
and
Comic Books

Edited by

Kat Kan

The Reference Shelf
Volume 82 • Number 5
The H.W. Wilson Company
New York • Dublin
2010

The Reference Shelf

The books in this series contain reprints of articles, excerpts from books, addresses on current issues, and studies of social trends in the United States and other countries. There are six separately bound numbers in each volume, all of which are usually published in the same calendar year. Numbers one through five are each devoted to a single subject, providing background information and discussion from various points of view and concluding with a subject index and comprehensive bibliography that lists books, pamphlets, and abstracts of additional articles on the subject. The final number of each volume is a collection of recent speeches, and it contains a cumulative speaker index. Books in the series may be purchased individually or on subscription.

Library of Congress has cataloged this serial title as follows:

Graphic novels and comic books / edited by Kat Kan.
    p. cm. — (The reference shelf ; v. 82, no. 5)
 Includes bibliographical references and index.
 ISBN 978-0-8242-1100-4 (alk. paper)
 1. Comic books, strips, etc.—History and criticism. 2. Graphic novels—History and criticism. I. Kan, Katharine.
 PN6710.G736 2010
 741.5'09—dc22

               2010034209

Cover: Portrait of three people standing in front of an urban skyline with a helicopter (Steve & Ghy Sampson/Getty Images).

Visit H.W. Wilson's Web site: www.hwwilson.com

Printed in the United States of America

Contents

Preface

Comics, graphic novels, sequential art—whatever one wishes to call them, books in the graphic format have gained unprecedented legitimacy. Once dismissed as ephemeral trash—mere kids' stuff—graphic novels now win literary awards and appear on *The New York Times* bestseller list. They are also finding their way into classrooms and school and public libraries, where they share shelf space with more traditional forms of literature.

The origin of the term "graphic novel" causes debate among comics fans and scholars, but Will Eisner's landmark *A Contract with God*, published in 1978, is most often cited as the first time the term and the form came together. While some artists and fans take issue with the label, it has become a catchall for numerous types of books—everything from splashy superhero anthologies and Japanese manga to harrowing Holocaust memoirs.

The articles collected in this volume of The Reference Shelf provide an overview of this wildly diverse, increasingly popular, and widely accepted form of literature. The writers range from comics industry insiders and scholars to newbie reporters suspicious of the form. Selections in the first chapter, "Up, Up, and Away: The Rise of Graphic Novels," touch on the history of comics and chart the format's rise in popularity in libraries, classrooms, and elsewhere. Just as Scott McCloud employed the format itself in his acclaimed book *Understanding Comics*, two of the included articles utilize comics to convey information to the reader.

The second chapter, "Out of the 'Comics Ghetto': Graphic Novels as Serious Literature," includes articles that describe the increasing acceptance of graphic novels as literature. Many entries cite Art Spiegelman's Pulitzer Prize-winning *Maus* and Alan Moore's deconstruction of the superhero genre, *Watchmen*, as groundbreaking graphic novels that tackle serious subjects and go well beyond the biff-bang-pow action most often associated with comics.

Educators at all levels are realizing the potential of graphic novels to enhance the reading skills of their students. Pieces in the third chapter, "Comics in the Classroom: Using Graphic Novels to Improve Literacy," explore this phenomenon.

Librarians have played a large role in legitimizing comics, and selections in the fourth chapter, "Graphica in the Stacks: The Role of Librarians," examine how they've done so, both in school and public libraries. In addition to acting as gate-keepers and selecting the material that makes it to the shelves, librarians can actively promote graphic novels by creating book clubs and hosting informational meetings.

The fifth and final chapter, "The People Behind the Pencils: Conversations with Artists," features interviews with renowned comic creators Art Spiegelman, Lynda Barry, Marjane Satrapi, Howard Cruse, Alison Bechdel, Daniel Clowes, and Gene Luen Yang. The artists discuss their work habits and inspirations, revealing how they use words and pictures to express their unique views of the world.

The pieces in this book range from newspaper articles and scholarly essays to on-line journal and blog entries. Together, they explain how and why graphic novels have gained such a prominent place in libraries and schools—both as popular reading materials and vital additions to educational curricula. While some prose purists continue to question the validity of graphic novels, the articles in this book offer proof of the form's literary merits.

I thank Joseph Miller, Ray Barber, Kenneth Partridge, Richard Stein, and Paul McCaffrey of H. W. Wilson, for giving me the opportunity to work with my favorite reading material, which allows me to say I get paid to read comics. And I send a special thanks to Dorothy Broderick, cofounder of *Voice of Youth Advocates*, who first encouraged me to write about graphic novels in libraries.

Katharine "Kat" Kan
October 2010

1

Up, Up, and Away:
The Rise of Graphic Novels

Editor's Introduction

In their stapled, serialized, newsstand form, comics were long dismissed as light and insubstantial. It wasn't until 1978, when Will Eisner published the long-form landmark *A Contract with God*, that critics and scholars began to see comics as more than frivolous pamphlets. In a bid to be taken seriously by publishers, Eisner labeled the book a "graphic novel," a term now used to describe various types of book-bound comics. The selections in this chapter chart the rising popularity of the graphic novel and its acceptance as a valid form of literature.

In "The Graphic Novel Silver Anniversary," this section's lead article, Andrew D. Arnold uses *A Contract with God* as a starting point for his discussion of the form. Arnold highlights many of the important artists that have followed in Eisner's footsteps and explains why "graphic novel" is a problematic term.

Next up, writer and artist Jessica Abel uses comic-book panels and word balloons to answer her piece's titular question: "What is a 'Graphic Novel'?" Abel originally published the cartoon on the Web site Artbomb.net, and she continues to make it available for educational use at Artbabe.com.

In "Drawing Power," self-styled "Prose Guy" Bob Thompson decides to give graphic novels a chance. He attends "SPLAT! A Graphic Novel Symposium," held in New York City, and interviews numerous industry luminaries, including creator and theorist Scott McCloud; *New Yorker* art director and Toon Books cofounder Françoise Mouly; cartoonists Adrian Tomine and Chris Ware; John Shableski of Diamond Book Distributors; and First Second Books' editorial director Mark Siegel. Artist Jonathan Bennett contributes several comic strips that illustrate Thompson's efforts—successful, ultimately—to embrace the medium.

With "Notes from the Underground: Graphic Novels Come of Age—in Monterey County and Around the World," Walter Ryce visits the 2009 Alternative Press Expo, held in San Francisco, and interviews two Californian comic creators: Jeff Hoke, the man behind *The Museum of Lost Wonder*, and Belle Yang, whose *Forget Sorrow* is a memoir told in graphic-novel form. Ryce also discusses the dark themes explored in many of today's comics and touches on the "odd juxtapositions" created when librarians lump all graphic novels together and shelve superhero collections next to more adult-oriented works.

In "Graphic Novels Are New Horizon for Top Authors," the next selection, George Gene Gustines looks at the growing trend of prose authors turning to graphic novels. He discusses the two main types: graphic novel adaptations of published prose works, such as Stephenie Meyers' *Twilight*, and original graphic novels based on established prose fiction series, such as Janet Evanovich's *Troublemaker*.

The chapter's final piece, "A Comic-Book World," finds University of Memphis professor Stephen E. Tabachnick arguing that graphic novels aren't just a fad, but rather a reflection of modern society. Due to their exciting visuals and quick pacing, graphic novels offer readers "the advantages of both print and electronic media," Tabachnick writes. He predicts comics will continue to grow in popularity, particularly as the violent, unpredictable world continues to shake people's perceptions of reality and render less farfetched the fantastical storylines often associated with the form.

The Graphic Novel Silver Anniversary[*]

By Andrew D. Arnold
Time, November 14, 2003

"You mean like pornographic?" queried the startled librarian when I asked for help researching articles about graphic novels. She had never heard the term for book-length comics used before. It's admittedly a not very well-liked phrase. Even among comic-makers the term only gets grudging usage, mostly because any alternative would be even less recognized. But "graphic novels" in name and in form have reached their 25th anniversary in 2003. To mark the occasion TIME.comix has two-part coverage. This week we look into their history, controversy and recent extraordinary growth. Next week will be an "instant library" list of 25 graphic novels that shouldn't be missed.

Will Eisner's "A Contract with God," published in 1978, gets the credit for being the first graphic novel, though it was not actually the first long-form graphic story nor the first use of the phrase. It was, however, the first marriage of the term, which appeared on the cover, and the intent of "serious" comix in book form. "It was intended as a departure from the standard, what we call 'comic book format,'" Will Eisner recently told TIME.comix. "I sat down and tried to do a book that would physically look like a 'legitimate' book and at the same time write about a subject matter that would never have been addressed in comic form, which is man's relationship with God." Though the concept of a "graphic novel" had been brought up among comix fans during the 1960s, Eisner claims to have [. . .] come up with it independently, as a form of spontaneous sleight-of-hand marketing. "[The phrase] 'graphic novel' was kind of accidental," Eisner said. While pitching the book to an important trade-book editor in New York, says Eisner, "a little voice inside me said, 'Hey stupid, don't tell him it's a comic or he'll hang up on you.' So I said, 'It's a graphic novel.'" Though that particular editor wasn't swayed by the semantics, dismissing the book as "comics," a small publisher eventually took the project and put the phrase "A Graphic Novel" on the cover, thereby permanently cementing the term into the lexicon.

Even then the terminology didn't really fit. "A Contract with God," was actually four short stories and not like a traditional novel at all. Art Spiegelman, author of the comix Holocaust memoir "Maus," recalled when "Contract" first came out. "I liked one of the stories very much but it didn't register with me as having anything to do with what I had already climbed on my isolated tower to try to make, which was a long comic book that would need a bookmark." In the past 25 years the meaning of the phrase has only gotten hazier and less satisfying. Japanese manga, superhero collections, non-fiction, autobiography—all of these are "graphic novels," a term that now applies to any square-bound book with a story told in comics format. "The problem with the word 'graphic novel' is that it is an arguably misguided bid for respectability where graphics are respectable and novels are respectable so you get double respectability," Spiegelman says. Eisner himself dislikes the phrase, calling it a "limited term," and prefers "graphic literature or graphic story."

Either of those terms seems preferable to the striving, mostly-inaccurate "graphic novel." But some would argue against any such terminology. Chip Kidd, book designer and "graphic novel" editor at Pantheon, an imprint of the giant trade publisher Random House, loathes the ghettoizing of such books, starting with their name. "What I don't like is when we have to categorize everything in order to appreciate or understand it," he wrote in an email. "At Pantheon, we do not see these books as part of a 'line,' or a 'program' any more than we would books by Ha Jin or Stanley Crouch. They are simply books we want to publish that happen to use the form of visual narrative."

As a critic, though, I would argue that these types of books are fundamentally different from prose. Blurring the line between them would be charmingly quixotic at best and harmful at worst. That which distinguishes drawn books from prose is what we love about them. The Artistry is different—way beyond mere genre—and must be celebrated. In order to talk about the unique pleasures of drawn books we necessarily distinguish them from their text-only relatives.

But categorizing graphic novels goes beyond artistic semantics to the real bottom line—dollars and cents. Most big bookstores, like Barnes & Noble and Borders, put all the graphic novels together in one place. Trade bookstores have become an increasingly important outlet for comic publishers so the strategy for selling them on the floor has become critical. Should Superman, manga and "Maus," sit side by side? Chip Kidd, among many others, can't stand this. "I truly believe that Spiegelman's 'Maus' should be shelved next to Elie Wiesel and Primo Levi, not next to the X-Men. Maus is a Holocaust memoir first and a comic book second." Micha Hershman, the graphic novel buyer for the Borders bookstore chain has no such doubts. "The graphic novel is a format," he says. "We would not segment the category by splitting up the graphic novel section." According to Hershman, Borders' research shows the "demographics for 'Maus' overlap with the ones for Spider-Man," so that it is theoretically easier to lure the reader of one to the other than it is to lure a reader of Elie Wiesel to "Maus."

Something seems to be working because graphic novels have finally reached a point of critical mass in both popular consciousness and sales. Jim King, VP of Sales and Service at Nielsen Bookscan, a book sales monitoring service, says that, based on preliminary research, sales for graphic novels have increased "exponentially." Micha Hershman at Borders confirms the trend, saying, "over the last four years graphic novels have shown the largest percentage of growth in sales over any other book category." English-translated Japanese comics, or manga, are chiefly responsible for this growth, according to Hershman. More specifically, manga aimed at girls, called shojo, have exploded. "Superheroes are up a little," says Hershman, " Alternative comics are up a little. But 60% of all Border's graphic novel sales are shojo."

Comic specialty shops have felt the up-tick too. Nick Purpura, a manager at Jim Hanley's Universe, a comic store in New York City, also reports an annual increase in graphic novel sales, most particularly in manga. Could graphic novels eventually make the traditional comic book disappear? Frank Miller, author of "The Dark Knight Returns," recently shocked a comics industry crowd at the annual Eisner awards by pronouncing the format to be a goner, declaring, "Our future is not in pamphlets." Nick Purpura disputes this, saying, "the serialized versions pay for the trades. That way publishers get to sell it twice—once to comics fans and again to people who only buy collections." Even so, he says, "books that sold marginally as comics sell better as graphic novels." Additionally, there have been an increasing number of "original graphic novels," as Purpura calls them, which never appeared in serialized form. The most impressive example of these is DC comics' October release of "Sandman: Endless Nights," by Neil Gaiman, which reached number 20 on the New York Times bestseller list.

The future of the graphic novel seems both sunny and dim. As a term for a kind of book, "graphic novel" has become increasingly dissatisfying. "Maybe for a short window it was enough to say 'graphic novel' but soon it won't be," says Art Spiegelman, "because if you talk about [Chris Ware's] 'Jimmy Corrigan' as a graphic novel you'll have to explain that it's not manga or Marvel. Then you are left saying, 'well it's got a seriousness of purpose' that the phrase 'graphic novel' alone won't offer." On the positive side, the public awareness of these books has vastly increased, creating a kind of renaissance era of intense creativity and quality. Says Spiegelman, "Ultimately the future of the graphic novel is dependent on how much great work gets produced against all odds. I'm much more optimistic than I was that there's room for something and I know that right now there's more genuinely interesting comic art than there's been for decades and decades."

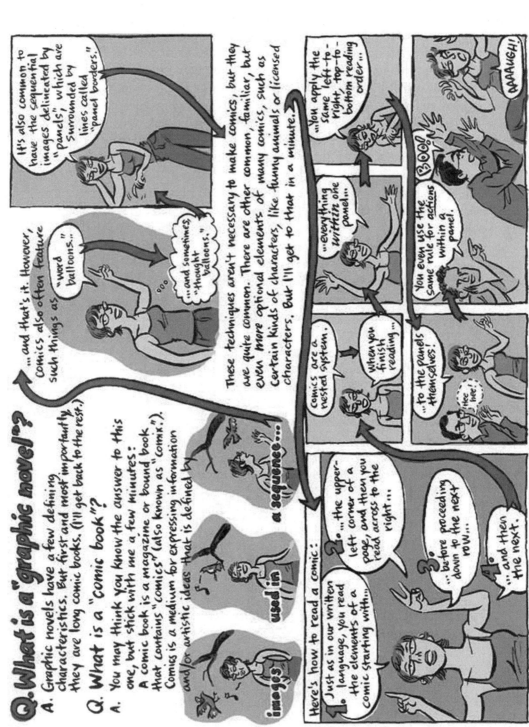

Created and illustrated by Jessica Abel (artbabe.com).

Article by Jessica Abel from Artbomb.net. Created, written and illustrated by Jessica Abel (www.jessicaabel.com, www.dw-wp.com) Twitter: dwandwp

You think you're funny, huh?

Hee! Hee!

I'll deal with you later!

"Wait a minute," you may be saying, "what ABOUT those superheroes?"

Ahem.

OK. "Comics" is the name of a medium, like "film" or "painting."

You don't think "film" means movies about gangsters, or cowboys, do you? Film is a way to express ideas. Any ideas you want to express.

OK. So what is a "graphic novel," besides a comic book?

Well, "graphic" means "told in images," not "naughty pictures."...

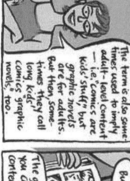

But "novel" is used less precisely. The term "graphic novel" is often applied to short-story collections as well.

I think "novel" is just used to mean "long book."

I don't know why.

Comics is like that. It's a container for ideas.

Heroic science fiction

Mmm...

Literary fiction

Hardcover or softcover, graphic novels have pages enough to need a square spine...

The term is also sometimes used to imply adult-level content — i.e. "comics are kids' stuff," but graphic novels are for adults." But then, sometimes they call long kids' comics "graphic novels," too.

Not a lot of vitamins in this kind, but you get a taste for it.

TASTE MY SWEET OCTOPUS!

My favorite flavor!

I'm done talking about it.

OK, let's stop.

delicious and nutricious!

But don't worry...

...so they can sit on the shelf with your other books.

The great thing about comics is, you can get an idea of their content just by flipping them open!

Drawing Power[*]

By Bob Thompson
The Washington Post, August 24, 2008

I've wandered into an alternative universe, and I'm trying to decide if I want to stay. The setting is the lovely, old-fashioned library of the General Society of Mechanics and Tradesmen, in midtown Manhattan. The event is a gathering called "SPLAT! A Graphic Novel Symposium." I'm here because the organizers have promised to lay out, in the course of a single day, "Everything You Ever Wanted to Know About Graphic Novels."

What I want to know is: How did this formerly ghettoized medium become one of the rare publishing categories that's actually *expanding* these days?

"SPLAT!" seems a perfect place to start looking for answers.

Sponsored by the New York Center for Independent Publishing, it's crammed with influential cartoonists, editors, agents, librarians, marketing types and booksellers. There will be talk of literary comics, autobiographical comics, Web comics, kids' comics, comics in libraries, comics in schools and much, much more. By day's end, my head will be buzzing with new knowledge on subjects ranging from the distribution revolution that helped make the graphic novel boom possible to the Manga Invasion from Japan.

Above all, "SPLAT!" is filled with enthusiastic voices.

What is a graphic novel?

"It's a perfect synthesis of artwork and literature!"

When will graphic novels come into their own?

"We seem to be in a golden age of comics publishing right now!"

And yet . . .

To a lifelong Prose Guy, whose idea of a good time involves a comfortable couch and a book full of nothing but words, the graphic novel galaxy can still feel far, far away.

Yes, I *know* comics can be ambitious and aimed at adults. Art Spiegelman's "Maus" made this indisputable two decades ago, and there has been plenty of impressive work done since. But I can't help wondering, even as I begin to explore the rise of what's sometimes called "sequential art," if I can ever overcome my personal bias toward prose.

Maybe Scott McCloud will help me sort this out.

I've been looking forward to the final "SPLAT!" offering, in which the man billed as "one of the great theorists of comics" will be holding forth. McCloud made his name 15 years ago with "Understanding Comics," a groundbreaking deconstruction of the cartoonist's art that itself takes the form of a 215-page graphic novel.

It's not really a novel, of course.

"Graphic novel" is "a goofy term," McCloud tells his listeners. "The first graphic novel that got a lot of play was Will Eisner's 'Contract With God.' The thing's an anthology. The next graphic novel that got a lot of play was 'Maus,' and it's a memoir. There are very few graphic novels that are actually graphic novels.

"What they are is a publishing shorthand that says: big fat comic with a spine— and people get that."

Now McCloud is taking audience questions, and here comes one that seems aimed in my direction.

What about those still-numerous naysayers, he is asked, who resist the idea that books filled with word balloons should be taken as seriously as pure prose? Isn't there a way to educate those annoying old fogies—perhaps through some kind of "adult literacy campaign for comics"?

Sounds good to me. After all, isn't education what I'm here for?

McCloud offers a different perspective. Some people will *never* get it, he says. "And it's okay. They'll die."

'A WHOLE LOT OF LITTLE SEESAWS'

It's easy to forgive McCloud a bit of coldblooded glee at the rising status of his art form. All you have to do is think back to how utterly unappreciated it was—in this country, at least—when he was launching his career a quarter-century back.

"We have to remind ourselves once in a while just how incredibly fast this has all happened," he says. It hasn't been that long since trying to interest American publishers in graphic novels was "beating what looked like a dead horse." Suddenly, seven years ago, "the horse opened its eyes. And then, like 7,000 horses came over the hill."

The numbers bear him out.

In 2001, the first year it started tracking them, the pop culture business Web site ICv2 reported a total of $75 million in graphic novel sales in the United States and Canada. By 2007, that total had quintupled, to $375 million, and graphic novels had gained their reputation as one of the few growth areas in publishing. As a result, every publisher in New York—they may be late adapters, but they're not blind—seemed to be scrambling for a piece of the action.

What happened?

A lot of things, I will discover. Best-selling ideamonger Malcolm Gladwell famously argued that you can often find a single, crucial "tipping point" to explain such a change. But "SPLAT!" panelist Bob Mecoy—a New York literary agent who has found himself selling more and more graphic novels over the past few years—says that a better image, in this case, would be "a whole lot of little seesaws" tipping one after another.

"Maus" was an early one, Mecoy says. Few would disagree.

A few days after "SPLAT!" I find myself splashing through the rainy streets of SoHo toward the place that particular seesaw began to tip. I've got an appointment to meet Art Spiegelman's wife and collaborator, Francoise Mouly, in the same building where, 28 years ago, they launched the influential cartoon journal Raw, in which Spiegelman's masterpiece first appeared.

Mouly is a voluble woman in her early 50s who, despite having left France for New York in 1974, retains much of the charming accent she arrived with. She mostly wants to tell me about her new publishing venture, Toon Books, a series of elegantly produced comic tales aimed at beginning readers. But her crowded studio feels like a museum of avant-garde cartooning—a blown-up cover of a Raw anthology dominates the back wall; a lovely old oak case holds "mechanicals" and color separations used eons ago to prepare work by the likes of Robert Crumb and Charles Burns for publication—and inevitably, the conversation slips into the past.

"There's a generation that grew up with Raw, which is strange for me," Mouly says, "because I'm like the old lady of comics!" As the art editor of the New Yorker, she is now in a position to pay her artists well. But she can recall a time when "the rewards were too few for anybody but insane people to actually want to be cartoonists."

Raw was created in large part to give these cartoonists, Spiegelman included, a place [where] their work could be seen. "Maus" was first published as a series of small booklets hand-glued into the magazine.

For those who haven't encountered the finished version, I can only urge you to check it out yourself. Attempts at description—"father and son angst," "Holocaust survival," "Jews as mice and Nazis as cats"—can't begin to convey the uncannily moving effect of Spiegelman's blend of words, pictures, intense themes and self-deflating humor. Published in two volumes by Pantheon, in 1986 and 1991, "Maus" made bestseller lists, won a 1992 Pulitzer Prize and established that a graphic novel could qualify as great literature.

What it did not immediately do, however, was help *other* graphic novels achieve similar commercial and literary prominence. As Mouly points out, some 15 years would pass between the publication of the first "Maus" volume and the beginning of the graphic-novel boom.

In the meantime, she and Spiegelman had a daughter and a son. And as the parents watched their children's very different progress toward reading, the seeds of Toon Books were sown.

"With our daughter," Mouly says, "you could hear the little wheels turning and the light bulb went up and boom, she was reading. With our son, you could hear the wheels turning—and nothing was happening."

They knew what to do, "which was to keep reading with him and make sure that reading is a pleasure." And they learned that what really held his attention was comics.

Spiegelman read him classics such as "Little Nemo" and "Krazy Kat." Mouly, who speaks French with her kids, read from the wide range of children's comics available in France. "It made me very aware," she says, how much they can be "a magic bullet at that moment." Comics give beginning readers a visual narrative to hold on to, "a thread through the labyrinth" that she thinks is even more important for children who *don't* have parents reading to them.

There was a supply problem, however.

American comics were now geared almost exclusively toward teens and young adults. "Oddly, as the medium grew," as Mouly and Spiegelman explain in the Toon catalogue they wrote together, "kids got left behind."

The couple's first impulse, in looking to correct this, was not to launch a line of books themselves but to work with an established company. Mouly says she shopped the concept "to every children's book publisher in town." Over and over, she was told: It's a great idea, but it won't work.

Why not?

It seems that an important seesaw hadn't yet tipped.

Bookstores need to know where to *put* things, Mouly explains. And publishers didn't want cartoon books aimed at beginning readers because "they didn't exist as a section in the store."

'THE "ULYSSES" OF COMICS'

Confession time: When I started on this self-education project, I'd barely read any graphic novels. It wasn't that I opposed the things on principle. It was just that—somewhat snobbishly—I didn't put them in the same category as *real* books.

Oh, I'd read "Maus" and been amazed by it. Much later, I read the similarly lauded memoir "Persepolis," by Iranian exile Marjane Satrapi, which vividly personalizes the tragedy of the Iranian revolution. But most graphic novelists remained just names to me, if that.

"I hear you're interviewing Adrian Tomine! You're so lucky!" a younger colleague burst out one day. Lucky indeed. I'd never heard of the guy 24 hours before.

Tomine turns out to be a gracious, articulate 30-something who has been drawing comics in some form or other since he was 4 or 5 years old. He offers himself as an example of the personality type drawn to "alternative" cartooning—i.e., work outside the superhero or funny pages mainstream—before there was money in it.

"If you talk to a lot of cartoonists," he says, you'll find "some sort of chaos or unsettled nature to their childhood," be it divorce (as in his case) or just "moving around a lot." Drawing comics "is so clearly some psychological way of taking life and ordering it into little squares that you can control."

His latest collection of little squares, "Shortcomings," carries a blurb from novelist Jonathan Lethem that compares Tomine's "mastery of narrative time" to that of short-story goddess Alice Munro. It's a complex fictional stew of relationships and ethnicity, and while I don't quite buy the Munro comparison, I'm captivated nonetheless. Tomine is published by a small but highly regarded Canadian outfit called Drawn & Quarterly, and I soon find myself bingeing on some of their other authors.

I find a lot to like. When I ask myself *why*, however, it's not easy to put the answer into words.

Take "Exit Wounds" by Israeli cartoonist Rutu Modan. An improbable love story built around a man's disappearance after a terrorist bombing, its "spare, affecting lines and charged dialogue add up to a tragicomic take on family and identity," according to The Post's reviewer. Fair enough, but most of that description could serve a prose novel just as well. What haunts me is the way Modan's lonely, angry lovers lock gazes across empty distance.

Or take Guy Delisle's "Pyongyang," a graphic memoir of his stint as an animator in totalitarian North Korea, and Joe Sacco's "The Fixer," a journalistic portrait of war-traumatized Sarajevo. As best I can tell, what elevates these very different nonfiction accounts are the same things that work in good, first-person prose: sharp-eyed observation, strong storytelling and a narrator who functions as the reader's guide. What seems different is the literal immediacy of the graphic versions. Within seconds, they can pull you into strange worlds.

At Tomine's suggestion, I read a graphic novel on another subject that I'd never, ever have expected to be addressed in this medium. Chester Brown's "Louis Riel: A Comic-Strip Biography" is a painstaking retelling, complete with footnotes, of the life of a "charismatic, and perhaps mad" 19th-century rebel against the Canadian government.

Talk about strange worlds! I'd never encountered Riel before. Brown makes him unforgettable.

Mid-binge, I realize that I should be setting aside my Drawn & Quarterly stack in order to prepare for an interview at Pantheon, the mainstream publisher most closely associated with quality graphic novels. My Pantheon to-read pile includes David B.'s "Epileptic," Charles Burns's "Black Hole" and—on the very top—Chris Ware's "Jimmy Corrigan: The Smartest Kid on Earth."

Legendary book designer and Pantheon comics guru Chip Kidd, the man I'm scheduled to meet, was responsible for acquiring Ware's book. He told Pantheon's sales force it was "the 'Ulysses' of comics." Hyperbole? Perhaps. But I know that

Ware is a huge talent. I also know that I really, really should read "Jimmy Corrigan" before I talk to Kidd.

So what's stopping me?

Well, I've noticed that Kidd has written a couple of novels himself. And by novels, in this case, I mean novels *without* pictures.

I pick up his latest, "The Learners." It's not "Ulysses," but it looks pretty good. Guess which book Prose Guy settles down with.

THE DISTRIBUTION FIX

John Shableski thinks graphic novels are Elvis, and he's not shy about saying so.

Shableski, 45, is an ultra-enthusiastic graphic novels marketer—favorite phrase: "How cool is that!"—for Diamond Book Distributors, based in Timonium, Md. Before joining Diamond last year, he was an ultra-enthusiastic graphic novels marketer at Brodart, a wholesaler to libraries. Before that he was a radio guy, and he's fond of music-business analogies.

"I always compare this to the beginning of rock-and-roll," he says. Tiny studios like Sun, Stax and Motown started cranking out "really great music" that forced the big boys to sit up and take notice. The same thing happened with independent comics publishers like Drawn & Quarterly, Fantagraphics and Dark Horse, which put out enough "really good books" to help rouse publishing's sleepy giants.

Yet putting out good books wasn't enough, Shableski explains over a grilled cheese sandwich at a Timonium diner. Other seesaws had to tip before the mainstream really woke up—and libraries were one of the earliest.

Shortly after he got hired at Brodart in 2003, he recalls, his boss handed him a stack of graphic novels ("Maus" and Mike Mignola's "Hellboy" among them) and said, "The libraries are asking about this stuff. I need you to figure this out." Naturally, Shableski started talking to librarians. Among the first was a Brodart consultant named Katharine Kan.

By phone from her home in Panama City, Fla., Kan, who's 53, tells me she's been an obsessive comics reader since she was "like, 6 years old." Her parents didn't mind, she says, because she read so many other things as well.

In the late 1980s, when libraries carried few comics of any kind, Kan had a job as a young adult services librarian in Hawaii. Amid constant complaints about "losing boys as readers around 10 or 11," she persuaded her boss to let her introduce Spider-Man, Batman and the like to the collection. Middle school boys began clustering around her desk. Soon she was branching out to Neil Gaiman's "Sandman" series and Stan Sakai's "Usagi Yojimbo."

Other librarians were discovering the comics effect as well: They saw both interest and circulation rise when they started adding graphic novels to their collections. In 2002, Michael Pawuk, a young adult services librarian from Cuyahoga County,

Ohio, helped organize a day-long program called "Get Graphic @ Your Library" as part of the American Library Association's summer conference.

"It was one of the best days of my life," says Pawuk, who helped recruit graphic novelists Spiegelman, Gaiman, Jeff Smith and Colleen Doran to talk to his information-hungry colleagues.

A few years later, Shableski left Brodart to join Diamond Book Distributors. In effect, he was jumping off one tipping seesaw and climbing on another, throwing his weight behind the effort to get more books with word balloons into bookstores.

And therein lies a complex but crucial tale.

To someone outside the business, it isn't obvious why selling graphic novels through bookstores should have been a particular problem. Hey, you put the things in your catalogue and send your reps around to chat up the booksellers, just as you would with any other books, right?

Wrong. Because until a few years ago, most comics publishers weren't in the habit of selling to bookstores *at all.*

There were a few exceptions (Gaiman's "Sandman" was one). But for the most part, these publishers—from the superhero factories DC and Marvel on down to the literary independents—were used to dealing with what's called the "direct market," meaning specialty stores devoted exclusively to comics. Mostly these stores featured "floppies" (individual comics), but they carried comics with spines as well.

At the time graphic novels first showed signs of booming, the direct market was monopolized—as it is today—by a single company: Diamond Comic Distributors. If you wanted to sell to comic stores, you had no real choice but to do so through the distributor's phone-book-size monthly catalogue. What's more, comics acquired through Diamond could not be returned. This meant that regular bookstores—accustomed to a distribution system under which they could send back unsold product—wanted nothing to do with them.

Recognizing this structural difficulty, Diamond itself started a separate book distribution arm and began hiring people like Shableski. But many comics companies chose to channel their bookstore efforts through mainstream publishers, who had more experience with bookstore distribution.

As manga stormed across the Pacific from Japan, for example, Simon and Schuster began distributing the No. 1 North American manga publisher, Viz, while HarperCollins made a deal to distribute rival Tokyopop. Among the independents, Drawn & Quarterly joined forces with Farrar, Straus and Giroux, while the Seattle-based Fantagraphics signed up with W.W. Norton.

"I don't think we would still be in business without the Norton deal," says Eric Reynolds of Fantagraphics—though he notes that the rise of the Internet as a distribution channel helped a great deal, too.

Shableski agrees that the distribution revolution was huge. But if you ask him to name the biggest recent change in the landscape, he points immediately to one more tipping seesaw.

"It's the major publisher involvement," he says. "Not just distributing, but creating original stories."

'ONE OF THOSE MOMENTS'

Mark Siegel personifies major publisher involvement. But this comes as a surprise even to him.

Siegel is the editorial director of First Second Books, a subsidiary of Macmillan, with offices in Manhattan's Flatiron Building. Not that long ago, he was an illustrator, designer and graphic novel true believer with big ideas but little hope of turning them into reality.

"I had these three sheets of paper I was carrying around, called 'A Vision for Graphic Novels in America,'" he says, thinking back four years to when he first encountered his current employers. "I was dreaming, basically."

Simon Boughton, who runs Macmillan's Roaring Brook Press, was one of the executives who heard Siegel's pitch. "It was one of those moments when you have a trend in the marketplace," Boughton says. Graphic novels were poised to jump "from being a niche business into being a mainstream publishing business."

But to make that jump, "you need a creative vision." And here was Siegel, offering one.

Like Mouly, Siegel grew up in France, which broadened his thinking about what is possible in comics. A cornerstone of his vision involved tapping into "a highly international talent pool," though with a strong American element. He also wanted to emphasize quality, target books at all different ages and offer "the best possible home for creators."

One creator he offered a home was Gene Luen Yang, whose "American Born Chinese" went on to become a 2006 National Book Award finalist—the first graphic novel to be so honored—and to win the American Library Association's prestigious Printz award for young adult literature. Other early titles included Grady Klein's "The Lost Colony" series ("An Asterix for America") and J.P. Stassen's "Deogratias," an intense evocation of the Rwandan genocide.

First Second gets high marks among most of the graphic novel types I talk with. But I also hear some criticism, which comes in two basic categories:

The first: It's too commercial.

The second: It's not commercial *enough*.

Two years after the imprint's launch, it remains a work in progress. What drives a publishing business, Boughton says, "is not categories, it's individual books." And however many quality titles one publishes, there's always a need for "a success that moves the needle." Hence the hopes both he and Siegel place in "Prince of Persia," due out this fall. Based on a popular video game, soon to be a Disney film, it has, Boughton says, "a lot of mass market chops."

Meanwhile . . .

Around the same time Siegel was dreaming his graphic dream, a young woman named Janna Morishima got herself hired at Scholastic, the children's book powerhouse, as "basically a glorified receptionist." She, too, developed a vision of the graphic future.

"I just got it in my head that we need to start a comics imprint at Scholastic," Morishima says.

Before long, she and her boss, David Saylor—who shared Morishima's interest and was well aware of the industry buzz—had collaborated on a memo proposing just that. As part of this effort, Morishima "made a pilgrimage to Forbidden Planet" and asked the folks at the famed New York comics emporium what they would recommend for an 8-year-old boy. They mulled a bit, then pointed her toward "Bone," an all-ages comic series that was successfully self-published for years by its creator, Jeff Smith.

Starring three blob-like cousins (they look like refugees from "Pogo" who've stumbled into "The Lord of the Rings"), "Bone" manages to come off as simultaneously epic and funny. And from a children's publisher's point of view, it has a crucial advantage over most independent work: It lacks the edgy adult content—explicit sex! graphic violence! alienation!—that scares off parents. Scholastic used a colorized, nine-volume version to launch its new Graphix imprint in 2005.

There are now 2.5 million copies in print.

Meanwhile . . .

Bob Mecoy, the agent who offered the "whole lot of little seesaws" metaphor to explain the graphic novel boom, was hopping onto the publishing seesaw himself.

Mecoy started his agency in 2003, after spending a quarter century "on the editor's side of the desk." In the early 1990s, as editor in chief at Avon, he'd gotten his own graphic novels education when he published a Spiegelman-edited series called Neon Lit. But that was almost a decade before the boom, and as an agent, he assumed he'd be peddling prose.

One day, however, he was approached by a couple of pediatricians who said: "We want to do the next 'What to Expect When You're Expecting.'" Visions of perpetual sales danced in his head. What could he do, he asked himself, to make the project appeal to the visually oriented young?

BINGO! GRAPHIC NOVEL!

Mecoy's pediatricians ended up getting cold feet, but never mind: He soon found other graphic novels to sell. "Walking around and talking to anybody who will talk to me," he found that "all the commercial publishers were saying: Yeah, we should be doing this." But they didn't know how to talk to cartoonists. "Nobody knew how to get in."

Four years later, helping them has become close to half of Mecoy's business.

Simon and Schuster asked his advice about graphic novels for kids, and he ended up selling them on a historical series called "Turning Points" (a version of the "We

Were There" books I loved as a child, in which fictional boys and girls wind up in the middle of historical events). He's the agent working with John Wiley & Sons to repackage Shakespeare plays as manga. He has even dipped his toe into politics: Crown is doing a graphic take on this year's presidential campaign, to be called "08," by cartoonist Dan Goldman and Michael Crowley of the New Republic.

Summing up, Mecoy unearths a gardening metaphor.

Graphic novels are all about "hybrid vigor," he says. That's what you get when you cross two plants and the combined version "grows bigger and faster than either one of them."

'HEARTBREAK SOUP' MEETS 'FASHION HIGH'

A few weeks into this project, I'm reading absolutely nothing but big fat comics with spines, and my inner Prose Guy is getting cranky. For one thing, they're too darn *short*. I love being immersed in a narrative for days at a time, but even the fattest comics don't take more than a few hours to read.

Please, please, can't I take a break and dive into the new translation of "War and Peace" or, at the very least, curl up with the latest Venetian mystery by Donna Leon?

Nope. My stack of graphic novels keeps getting higher. And some are good enough to make my prose itch disappear.

By the end of "Blankets," Craig Thompson's lovely memoir of childhood and first love, I've forgotten its form and simply bought into the characters and the story. Cyril Pedrosa's "Three Shadows" tugs at my parental heartstrings with every swirling image of a broad-shouldered father fighting to save a small, doomed child.

To my surprise, I find myself wondering if Paul Karasik and David Mazzucchelli's version of Paul Auster's "City of Glass" might be *better* than Auster's original. To borrow the words of my smart brother-in-law, who lent me the adaptation, its "visual representations of intense states of mind" greatly magnify its emotional force.

And then there's Gilbert Hernandez's "Heartbreak Soup," a collection of everyday stories set in a fictional Central American hamlet called Palomar. Hernandez's work is part of a long-running Fantagraphics series called "Love and Rockets," created with his brother Jaime. I like it for the same reason I got hooked on Armistead Maupin's "Tales of the City" when the San Francisco Chronicle first serialized it: It's an addictive soap opera, replete with humor and heart.

All this reminds me of another tipping seesaw that, over the past couple of decades, helped pave the way for the graphic novel boom. Scott McCloud describes it in three words, with a lengthy pause between each:

"Comics. Got. Better."

Which is certainly true.

But I'm also reading far too many things that Prose Guy would have set aside after a few pages if finishing them weren't part of the job at hand.

Sometimes, as with "Bone," this is because years of reading to my kids has gotten me attached to a higher grade of children's literature. Smith's work is enjoyable enough, but it's not subtle. Sometimes, as with Scholastic's "Fashion High" series, I end up grinding my teeth the same way I would at a prose title that portrayed teen girls as universally obsessed with consumerism and popularity.

Are there smart new takes on superheroes out there? Undoubtedly, but I don't have the patience to track them down. After a few unhappy attempts, I accept that I'm just not a superheroes kind of guy. Is there merit to graphic bestsellers like Frank Miller's "300" and "Sin City"? Perhaps, but I'm too blinded by all the testosterone to see it.

As for "Prince of Persia," for which the nice folks at First Second have such high hopes, I regret to report that it seems to me *both* too commercial and not commercial enough. Reading it, I found myself longing for a copy of "The Arabian Nights."

'WE JUST COULDN'T KEEP THE STUFF ON THE SHELVES'

"BOOF!! . . . SHWIP!! . . . ONNNNG!! . . . GUH!! . . . THOOOM!! . . . URAAAAAH!!"

Finally, I've bitten the manga bullet. I'm making my way through Volume 19 of "Naruto," the most popular manga series in the world.

I'm getting used to the idea of reading Japanese-style, from back to front and right to left. I'm liking the variation in cartoon noises manga offers. And I'm doing my best to set aside Prose Guy's bias against endless combat sequences involving giant snakes and frogs, not to mention characters who pause mid-battle to say things like "I cut off his heart's keirakukei . . . the chakra network he heals himself with from the power of nine-tails."

There's no getting around it, however: The world's most popular manga is making me nostalgic for "Fashion High."

If you're wondering, at this point, precisely how manga is defined, you shouldn't be embarrassed. I keep asking knowledgeable people that question, and I get a wide range of answers. Some people talk about the cinematic fluidity of manga as opposed to the more painterly nature of Western comics. Others mention stylistic tics many manga artists share (wide eyes, particularly). But mostly they define manga as "Japanese comics," nothing more.

"Manga isn't a style of art," Kurt Hassler explains. "It's every bit as diverse as American comics."

Hassler should know. At 35, he's the co-founder of a new Hachette imprint, Yen Press, that mostly publishes manga. More important, in his previous life as a buyer at Waldenbooks and then Borders, he was as responsible as anyone for creating the manga sections you now see in chain bookstores: aisles filled with teens, often seated on the floor, flipping through volumes from series like "Fruits Basket," "Naruto," "Death Note" and "Bleach."

When he started in 1998, Hassler says, "Graphic Novels was a tiny, tiny category" at Waldenbooks, with maybe 10 titles on a single shelf: Alan Moore's "Watchmen," Frank Miller's "Batman: The Dark Knight Returns," a scattering of "Star Wars" adaptations, a couple of Neil Gaiman's books. "That was all that was crossing over."

What? No "Maus"?

" 'Maus' was in Holocaust Studies."

Hassler got hooked on Japanese visual culture as a teenager. A decade later, he pushed Waldenbooks to start carrying popular manga titles like "Sailor Moon," and before long, "we just couldn't keep the stuff on the shelves."

Manga's rise was so rapid that it now rivals established categories like science fiction, fantasy and romance in terms of bookstore space. Its success helped the broader graphic novel category as well. Because manga "turned" so fast, it gave buyers like Hassler and his Barnes and Noble counterparts "the financial ability to get other graphic novels in."

One result was that it accelerated their migration from specialty stores to the mainstream.

In 2001, near the beginning of the manga explosion, pop culture business Web site ICv2 estimated $32 million in bookstore sales of graphic novels as compared with $43 million in comic shop sales. In 2007, the bookstore number was $250 million while comic shops did half that.

It occurs to me that if you had to pick the single tipping seesaw most responsible for the graphic novel boom, manga might be the one. I'm also fascinated by the gender breakthrough it represents. Readers of American comics, especially the superhero genre, are "90 percent boys," Hassler says, but manga—many of whose popular series combine action with relationship drama—"is more like a 50-50 split."

I learn more from a conversation with Daniel Pink.

A 43-year-old former Al Gore speechwriter, Pink is best known as the author of "Free Agent Nation" and "A Whole New Mind," a pair of books about the changing American economy. Oddly enough, however, he's also the man behind what his publisher has been hyping as the first American business manga ever.

Over coffee at a Starbucks on Wisconsin Avenue, he tells me how he came to write "The Adventures of Johnny Bunko: The Last Career Guide You'll Ever Need."

Intrigued by manga's penetration of the United States, Pink won a fellowship to study the "manga industrial complex" that dominates Japanese pop culture. Thinking he might produce some kind of manga himself, he came up with a story line involving a supernatural sprite named Diana—summoned by the snapping of magic chopsticks—whose mission it is to teach the title character "the most important lessons of a satisfying, successful career."

Speaking of lessons: Pink learned that "manga is very much about speed." So he made sure "Johnny Bunko" could be read in an hour or less.

He learned that in Japan, "twenty-two percent of printed material is manga." To help me grasp its mind-boggling ubiquity, he suggests that I imagine the Tenley Mini Market, just down the street, filled with "huge stacks of weekly comic magazines, more prevalent than Time or Newsweek or—dare I say it—The Washington Post."

But the most important thing Pink learned was that in America, we have a "restricted, constricted view" of what comics can be.

"In Japan, you can get manga for how to deal with your finances, how to find a mate, cooking, history of Buddha, whatever," he says. If you're working in the medium, "you can do really good stuff, you can do really bad stuff. You can do sports, you can do documentaries. You can do gripping narratives, you can do cheesy narratives."

In other words, in the world of Japanese comics, you can do anything you want.

'IT'S A MEDIUM, NOT A GENRE'

Anything. You. Want.

We're not quite there yet on this side of the Pacific, but we're working on it.

And when it comes to the future of graphic novels in the United States, there may be no one with as inclusive a vision as Hill and Wang publisher Thomas LeBien.

LeBien is the man who greenlighted veteran comics guys Sid Jacobson and Ernie Colon when they pitched him a project many saw as impossibly strange: a graphic novel version of the 9/11 report. Hill and Wang published it in 2006—successfully, to wide acclaim—but LeBien has tired of hearing what an astonishing feat this was.

"There wasn't a review or a comment about that book," he says, "that didn't have the opening paragraph saying 'Look what comic books are doing now!'" But this "golly gee" reaction ran counter to his own view, which was that "we're a visual society and have been for many years."

When LeBien looks into the future, he sees the graphic medium breaking free from the "straitjacket" traditional categories impose. Among his challenges: "How do I bring a current-events book buyer to this format? How do I bring somebody who bought Tom Friedman to buy a graphic novel?"

But he's not just talking about current events.

Besides the 9/11 adaptation, he's already published graphic biographies of Malcolm X, Ronald Reagan and J. Edgar Hoover, with an eye to the school and library markets. Sure he's signed up Jacobson and Colon to do "After 9/11," which will tell the story of the war that followed the attacks, but he also has high hopes for "The United States Constitution: A Graphic Adaptation." There will be an introduction to genetics, a biography of dancer Isadora Duncan, a history of Vietnam . . .

"It's a *medium*, not a *genre*" has become a kind of mantra in the comics world, and it's one LeBien wholeheartedly embraces. The subjects you could treat effectively in a graphic novel are "almost limitless," he says. And many "are going to come from quarters that will be utterly unpredicted and unpredictable."

Meanwhile, as a brand new father, there's one thing he can imagine: "The person who brings out the graphic novel equivalent of 'What to Expect When You're Expecting' " is sure to make a killing.

Wait! Haven't I heard that before?

Maybe it's time for Prose Guy to wrap things up.

My stack of graphic novels seems undiminished, though I've been through dozens of them. I've fully absorbed the "anything you want" lesson and I know there's more and more good work out there that's to my taste (along with much that isn't). I've seen the future of graphic novels—hey, they'll be vamping their way into our cellphones any minute, just like everything else—and I know there's a generation coming of age for whom sequential art will seem as familiar as video games.

But I've also learned that alternative universes can make you homesick. So I'm going to head back to the prose planet now.

It's a place where you get to illustrate stories with whatever images your inner graphic novelist dreams up.

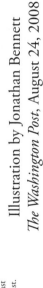

Illustration by Jonathan Bennett
The Washington Post, August 24, 2008

Illustration by Jonathan Bennett

The Washington Post, August 24, 2008

Originally printed in *The Washington Post*, August 24, 2008. Reprinted with permission of the artist.

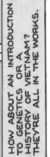

Illustration by Jonathan Bennett

The Washington Post, August 24, 2008

Notes from the Underground[*]

Graphic Novels Come of Age—in Monterey County and Around the World

By Walter Ryce
Monterey County Weekly, February 18–24, 2010

OH, WHAT A SCENE

Oct. 17–18, 2009, San Francisco's cavernous, airplane-hangar-like Concourse raised its industrial gate to one of the biggest independent comic book conventions in California, the Alternative Press Expo—a kind of Comic-Con for the odd and artsy—and in poured a capacity crowd, fanning out among the 325 comics artists, writers, publishers, sellers and distributors.

There were guys selling prints of Christopher Walken tinkering in a garage, building a robot while drinking a Tab. There was the girl who glued found objects onto construction paper, bound it, and presented each unique creation as a comic book. There was Drawn & Quarterly, a distributor from Montreal, hawking Dave Eggers and Robert Crumb. Jeff Smith, artist and writer behind *Bone*, a 5-million-selling, 1,300-page epic of a fable, was there, as was Phoebe Gloeckner, 2008 Guggenheim Fellow and creator of the brutally frank *The Diary of a Teenage Girl*, and Monterey's Bridgett Spicer of the comic strip *Squid Row*.

Anime chicks and skater dudes, earnest geeks and pierced co-eds, art schoolers and anxious fans were all there. And Jeff Hoke. He was there, too.

He stood out. Not so much because he was older than the prevailing demographic of those two days, or that he looked serene jammed in the bustling marketplace of vendors, but because his book and his booth looked so much better than the raw get-ups around him. His book was filled with arcane stuff, but meticulously executed, a fully realized hybrid of words, illustrations and layout.

In his own way, Hoke embodied the growing stature of APE's art form, which spans generations, and has gained momentum in the move from obscure subculture to piercing niches in the mainstream. Though he's part of a genre that's growing, Hoke admits he's still got some ways to go.

"APE is not [entirely] my crowd," he said. "I'm a fringe of a fringe of a lot of different groups: retired architects, psychologists, weird old guys."

When asked where he's from, Hoke replied, "Monterey."

GETTING LOST IN THE WONDER

There's this museum outside a city, a hulking stone fortress of Egyptian motifs, Greek columns and Art Deco shapes, guarded by two sentinel statues: a dragon straddling a globe and a bald baby, arms folded. Up its steps, across its castle-like threshold, lies a vast, circular lobby, lined with arches embedded with statues of seven Muses including Calliope, the Muse of Epic Poetry. The floor is a swirling pattern of fractals emanating from a circle that contains a triangle that contains a circle enscribed with the Latin words *gravitas*, *miraculum* and *levitas* (gravity, wonder, levity). There's a front desk and a map to the seven exhibition halls of the *Museum of Lost Wonder*. To continue the journey into this arcane world of science and mysticism, one just needs to turn the page.

Hoke conceived, wrote and illustrated *The Museum of Lost Wonder*—a 160-page tour through his imaginary museum, inspired by 16th and 17th century invention, alchemy and philosophy—while serving for the last 16 years as the Monterey Bay Aquarium's senior exhibit designer. There, he's led the building of the Splash Zone, MBARI's Mission to the Deep exhibit and a global warming exhibit coming in March.

"I get paid to build other people's ideas," he says months after APE, in his modest, third-floor apartment near Cannery Row. A bookshelf grazes the ceiling, heavy with tomes like *Anatomy of the Psyche: Alchemical Symbolism in Psychotherapy* by the Jungian Edward F. Edinger. In glasses and brown leather jacket, Hoke's dressed like a retired Indiana Jones, though his red hair conjures an older, more studious Conan O'Brien. "I needed to work on my own ideas. With [*The Museum*], I could do anything. It's a memory palace to put all the ideas I had as a kid."

Though *The Museum of Lost Wonder* is appointed with pictures of kids who demonstrate hands-on projects, and cut-outs with which to build models of buildings that look like dioramas of ancient monuments, it primarily appeals to the adult intellect and sense of wonder, to a time when science didn't explain all, leaving room for the imagination. "The kid in adults," Hoke puts it. "I like the time period when science was personal. Curiosity cabinets filled with watches, shells, machines next to what they thought were unicorn horns."

Ten years in the making, the book compiles Hoke's fascination with the mix of emerging science and ancient mysticism during the Age of Enlightenment, and omnivorously absorbs ideas from Carl Jung, Edinger, Galileo, Aristotle, Buddha, cosmology, epistemology, ontology. Its seven chapters, named after the stages of the process of alchemy, including Calcinatio (fire) and Sublimatio (air), open with a full-page drawing of each fantastical exhibit hall, followed by written exposition, exercises, icons and insets that elaborate the principles of each process as they relate to myth, philosophy, history and science. The Calcinatio chapter covers fire as creation myth, fire as Big Bang theory, fire as the "aha" moment of clarity. "Try this with a friend," reads the exercise. "No tools required."

The elaborate drawings are modeled after classical etchings like Gustave Doré's *Illustrations for Paradise Lost*. The illustrations of kids demonstrating the exercises are a wry homage, sourced to the Dover Publications and *How and Why Wonder Books* of Hoke's childhood.

It's an intriguing, rich work, so it's a wonder it isn't more widely available locally; Hoke says the Seaside Public Library carries it, and it's available for purchase at his own website, www.lostwonder.org. "I'm doing WonderCon at San Francisco's Moscone Center in April," he says. "It's like [San Diego's] Comic-Con North. My audience is just not here [in Monterey]. It's in the city."

Because his book is a hard-to-define anomaly, it settles, maybe uneasily, in . . .

THE REALM OF GRAPHIC NOVELS

A man who calls himself Night Owl reclines on his sofa to watch TV with a woman who calls herself Silk Spector II. Old friends and teammates, the two begin to kiss and disrobe to make love. But without his costume and gadgets, Night Owl—real name Daniel Dreiberg—feels psychologically impotent, and his body follows suit.

A woman and three children, all Jews living in the Nazi-imposed ghetto of Srodula in Poland, discover that the Gestapo is rounding up everyone for transport to Auschwitz. "I won't go to their gas chambers," she says. "And my children won't go to their gas chambers." She poisons the children and herself.

A shy, Christian teenage boy at Bible camp meets a girl who shares his fidelity to faith, but he finds more awakening inside him than spiritual kinship. His attraction to her first settles in when she sleeps and he can only look on in wonder.

These scenes come from the pages of *Watchmen*, *Maus* and *Blankets*—comics all, but of a different strata now commonly referred to as graphic novels.

Graphic novels have been called, variously, trade paperbacks, non-superhero comics, art comics and sequential art—the definition is still in contention. Even Merriam-Webster doesn't get it quite right: "a fictional story that is presented in comic-strip format and published as a book." Take out the word "fictional" and the definition veers closer to reality.

The term "graphic novel" is a signifier differentiating serials like *Archie*, *Boondocks* and *Superman* from long-form works like Joe Sacco's *Palestine*, a journalistic dispatch, in comic drawings, of conflict in the West Bank and the Gaza Strip.

In general, comic books are staple stitched while the thicker graphic novels are book bound; graphic novels are drawn in comics style but don't contain ads; a series of comics, book-bound, is a graphic novel; a graphic novel must have panels in a sequence, or else it's a picture book; finally, these rules are subject to change. (And probably will.)

ONCE UPON A TIME

The first Golden Age of comics occurred from the late 1930s to the late '40s, spawning *Superman, Batman, Captain America, The Spirit, Wonder Woman* and others. It ended around the time of the 1948 U.S. Senate Subcommittee on Juvenile Delinquency, 1950s McCarthyism and the subsequent restrictions of the Comic Code Authority, which regulated content—de facto censorship—for mainstream titles, denoted by a stamp-sized label on the cover. From the late '60s well into the '70s, underground comix (note the spelling) like *Fritz the Cat* by Robert Crumb and *The Fabulous Furry Freak Brothers* by Gilbert Shelton bucked the CCA by depicting stories of sex, drugs and counterculture mores. But they existed on the periphery; it wasn't until the late '80s that mainstream comics unshackled their pages from the restrictive codes.

"The Comics Code used to be on 90 percent of comics," says Bobby Gore, who opened Current Comics in Monterey and Salinas, which just celebrated its eighth anniversary this past Valentine's Day, on the advice of Sylvia Panetta. "Now, there's hardly any."

Justin Green can partly be credited for that. Paul Gravett, of *Graphic Novels: Everything You Need to Know*, writes that Green's 1972 *Binky Brown Meets the Holy Virgin Mary* was an "astonishing self-flagellation of Catholic guilt and obsessive-compulsive disorder" that freed Art Spiegelman and Robert Crumb to delve deeper into their personal lives and into taboo subjects.

In 1985, Will Eisner published *Comics and Sequential Art*, a treatise that approached the craft of comics as a serious medium, like film or painting, inviting writers and artists to strive for higher artistic aspirations. They did. Acclaimed comics writer Neil Gaiman described this new era—reflected in the graphic novels of today—as a "second Golden Age." A characteristic is that "non-superhero graphic novels" are primarily written for adults, the bigger, slicker books being priced out of reach of kids. Their stories are wildly diverse and mature, from Brian Fies' wrenching *Mom's Cancer* to Frank Miller's reimagined Batman in *The Dark Knight Returns* to—no lie—the *9/11 Report*.

R-E-S-P-E-C-T

Academia has been curiously, ever more enthusiastically, examining graphic novels. University of Illinois professor of library and information science, Carol L.

Tilley, is championing comics and graphic novels as a medium in their own right, one that can impart not just reading aptitude in the young, but a sophisticated, holistic grasp of artistic communication. Her argument is supported by studies released by the school last November.

Time magazine deemed the medium substantial enough to devote Andrew D. Arnold on a web column, time.comix, on it for five years (he signed off in 2007 with an article titled "The End").

"I noticed more media and researchers were citing Scott McCloud's *Understanding Comics*," says Jonathan Osburg, who teaches English at Monterey Peninsula College. "Andrea Lunsford at Stanford and Henry Jenkins at USC, formerly of MIT's Media Lab, were teaching [graphic novels]." The curriculum for Osburg's English 43 class, once shy of a full house but now filled to capacity with a waiting list, includes graphic novels by Scott McCloud (*Understanding Comics*), Alan Moore (*Watchmen*) and Neil Gaiman (*Sandman*). "We study mythology, conventions, how comics manipulate time, how it uses one sense—sight—to convey all five senses," Osburg says.

Monterey County Free Libraries counts hundreds of graphic novels in its collection, but the rapid evolution and vast variety of titles have created odd juxtapositions. At its Seaside branch, they are classified as "young adult," reside next to the children's section, and are labeled with a sticker with the word "BAM!" exploding like from a '60s *Batman and Robin* episode; but that sticker is also affixed to Fies' *Mom's Cancer*, whose cover depicts a woman, bald, neck bandaged, staring sleepily into a void.

A librarian at the Salinas Steinbeck Library winced at the prospect of carrying a popular title called *The Walking Dead*: "It's unbelievably violent."

Graphic novels are a Wild West of reading, traversing unchartered territory with soaring imagination, but also plunges into darker regions. Alan Moore is a literary giant within and outside of the genre, but his *V for Vendetta* practically advocates for terrorism against totalitarian governments. Robert Crumb's catalog, barring his faithful comic reproduction *The Book of Genesis*, is an id-run-amok blast of sex, neurosis and anger. Ariel Schrag's *Awkward and Definition*, poignant memoirs of her high school years, written while she was still in high school, contain detailed scenes of her experimentation with sex and drugs.

All this free expression has triggered push-back. Last year an Iowa man was convicted of possessing Japanese comics that were deemed "obscene visual representations of the sexual abuse of children," in violation of the 2003 Protect Act. It's the first conviction under that law for cartoon art, calling into question the artistic and literary merit and freedoms of the medium. Phoebe Gloeckner also drew the sexual abuse of a child—herself, at the hands of her step-father. It was done with detached irony masking seething anger, arriving at artistic catharsis. Could she, too, be convicted?

The caveat is "parents beware." The same rules that apply to Internet usage, video games, movies and TV when it comes to kids apply to graphic novels. But really the issue is moot. Today's non-superhero graphic novels are adults talking to other adults, with fidelity to their stories, not censors. If they contain sex, violence or subversive stuff, it's usually a reflection of the real world. Sacco's comics journalism in *Safe Area: Goražde*, about the Bosnian-Serbian war, portrays its cost in gruesome detail, but any protest over that is distraction from the real obscenity—the war itself.

ONWARD AND UPWARD

Though they accounted for one of the few publishing growth areas in recent years, graphic novels have suffered—and enjoyed—the same fringe status as many new variants of culture have, from Impressionism to beat poetry to hip-hop. Urban centers tend to embrace these new movements quickly, as evidenced by the thousands at the Alternative Press Expo. But the creative magnetism of graphic novels pulls them into further reaches. Current Comics, running an anniversary sale until Feb. 20, is going strong.

"Adventure Comics [closed shop] about three years ago," says Current Comics' Bobby Gore, "so we're the only ones left." (He says Adventure Comics once employed a Salinas youngster by the name of Greg Rucka, now counted as a giant in comics as the writer of titles like *Wolverine*, *Wonder Woman* and indie British serial *Queen & Country*.)

The Salinas Public Libraries have been a proponent of graphic novels. Last July, program managers Garland Thompson (a comics fan who describes them as morality tales) and Lori Wood assembled a series of events for Graphic Novels Month, including a visit and workshop by creators of an Asian-American comics anthology, *Secret Identities* (as reported in the Weekly's "Novel Graphics," July 16–22).

"Graphic novels circulate more than anything else," says librarian Bjorn Jones. "Movies drive it."

And vice versa. Chris Arrocena, who works at Current Comics in Salinas, says his grandfather, who read comic books while on tours of duty in Korea and Vietnam, told him, "Hollywood ran out of ideas and turned to comics."

Proof is plentiful: *Watchmen*, *Dark Knight*, *Ghost World*, *American Splendor*, *A History of Violence*, *Sin City*, *Coraline*, *300*, and on and on. Coming soon: *Ronin*, *Thor*, and *Y the Last Man*.

Seaside's Abe Wilson, age 35 and proprietor of madcowcards.com, says he usually buys at Current Comics, though he was found selectively browsing the plentiful stacks at Borders.

"My idea of decorating my home is books." Out of his library of about 4,000 books, he estimates graphic novels account for 250–300, and rising. "Serious authors can't ignore the genre anymore."

And they don't. Former *New York Press* columnist and author Jonathan Ames has entered the fray with *The Alcoholic*, a Bukowski-esque tale of the author's bouts with booze and drugs. Andrew James Thomas, a local co-facilitator and addictionologist, recommends it to his addicted patients, calling Ames "ballsy" and his story "raw."

Closer to home, children's book author, illustrator and Carmel resident Belle Yang has jumped into the vibrant arena (as have Deepak Chopra and Stephen King, while Michael Chabon turned in a Pulitzer Prize-winning novel about comics). She's created a soon-to-be-released graphic novel memoir about her father's family called *Forget Sorrow*. It's a natural medium for her, inspired by celebrated works like Marjane Satrapi's Iranian Islamic Revolution memoir, *Persepolis*. "The first [graphic novel] that made an impact on me was *Maus*," Yang says. "*Epileptic*, by David B. showed how you can visualize trauma from symbols and iconography—you don't have to draw the reality. Another book I loved was Alison Bechdel's *Fun Home*. It's extraordinarily literary, but moves at a fast clip."

Yang has chosen her influences wisely: *Maus* was awarded a Pulitzer, *Epileptic* won the 2005 Ignatz Award for Outstanding Art, while *Fun Home* was named best book of 2006 by *Time*, over Cormac McCarthy's *The Road*. Yang's own work took three years to complete.

"I put my whole energy, mental and physical, into this book. I feel like the book is my own flesh and blood . . . I think I'd like to do two more."

The future of graphic novels is being steered by the urgent stories and devoted craft of writers and artists like Belle Yang and Jeff Hoke, Alan Moore, Neil Gaiman and Frank Miller, Harvey Pekar, Kaja and Phil Foglio, and Daniel Clowes. But its future must also be aligned with a dedicated audience, one that's willing to seek and uncover lost wonders, like Hoke's book.

Abe Wilson has become a voracious reader of graphic novels in the last three years, but until a friend suggested *Watchmen*, *Preacher*, and *The Sandman*, he had been oblivious to the medium.

"It's not a movie, it's not a picture, it's not a novel," he says. "It has the strengths of cinema and the novel. As a medium, it has no limits; they have grown up." He waves his hand across the expanse of the Border's bookstore: "Every genre of fiction and non-fiction is represented in the medium of graphic novels. Even Strunk & White's *Elements of Style*."

Graphic Novels Are New Horizon for Top Authors[*]

By George Gene Gustines
The New York Times, February 8, 2010

Look! Up in the sky! It's a prose author moving a ton of graphic novels!

Last month, Yen Press announced that it would print 350,000 copies of a graphic-novel adaptation of "Twilight," the first part of the immensely popular vampire saga created by Stephenie Meyer. Now comes word from Dark Horse Comics that it will print 100,000 copies of a graphic novel by Janet Evanovich, the best-selling mystery writer, that will continue her "Motor Mouth" series of novels.

These are staggering initial print runs for graphic novels. More typical is a run of 20,000 to 25,000, which is usually enough for both the comic-book market and general bookstores, according to Milton Griepp, the publisher and founder of ICv2, an online trade publication that covers pop culture for retailers.

"Three hundred and fifty thousand is way higher than anything anybody's done that I'm aware of for a new graphic novel," Griepp wrote in an e-mail.

In August 2008, expecting a major sales bump from the film version of "Watchmen," DC Comics printed more than 900,000 copies of the softcover collected edition of the comic. According to Nielsen BookScan, which tracks bookstore sales, 733,000 copies of that edition were sold in 2008 and 2009 combined. More than 170,000 copies were sold in comic stores in those two years, according to estimates at ICv2.

"Watchmen," a dark tale by Alan Moore and Dave Gibbons, has been a perennial top seller since the limited series was first collected in 1987. In 2001, it sold around 22,000 copies; in 2007, it sold nearly 100,000.

"We were really pushing the boundaries for the history of the category, and with a property like 'Twilight,' it seemed justified," said Kurt Hassler, the publishing director for Yen Press.

When "Breaking Dawn," the fourth and final installment of the vampire saga, went on sale in 2008, publisher Little, Brown & Co. Books for Young Readers printed 3.2 million copies. To date, 45 million copies of the four "Twilight" books have been sold in the United States. If even a small percentage of this audience tries the graphic novel, the ambitious printing will seem like a safe bet.

"Twilight" will be split into two graphic novels. Hassler said Meyer was involved in "every panel of every page" of the adaptation, down to the dialogue balloons.

"The characters and settings are very close to what I was imagining while writing the series," Meyer said in a statement.

The first graphic novel, illustrated by Young Kim, a Korean artist, will be released March 16 as a $19.99 hardcover in the same trim size as the original novels.

In Evanovich's case, rather than an adaptation, "Troublemaker: A Barnaby Adventure" will be the third installment of a series, after her best-selling "Metro Girl" and "Motor Mouth" novels. These revolve around a NASCAR driver, Sam Hooker, and Alexandra Barnaby, a mechanic.

This two-part graphic novel is being written with Evanovich's daughter, Alexandra, a fellow comic-book fan. The first part will be released July 20 as a $17.99 hardcover. The second is due in the fall.

The authors collaborated closely with the book's artist, Joelle Jones, to convey their vision of the characters. "She finally just nailed it," Evanovich said.

An important goal for "Troublemaker" was to attract Evanovich's fan base to a new format. "We thought it was a great opportunity to expand the readership of graphic novels," said Michael Martens, the vice president for business development at Dark Horse Comics, an independent publisher.

As a result, the graphic novel is written as much for Evanovich's core readers as it is for comic-book fans.

Evanovich said she would love to see all her books turned into graphic novels.

The latest installment in Evanovich's Stephanie Plum series, "Sizzling Sixteen," is due out June 22 in hardcover with a print run of 2.5 million. The paperback editions of her "Motor Mouth" series had a run of roughly 1 million each.

Of the graphic-novel process, Evanovich said she marveled at the end results.

"The script was the structure, but it almost disappears," she said. "All those words that we labored over are now in bubbles over characters' heads. The book becomes the action and the pictures."

A Comic-Book World*

By Stephen E. Tabachnick
World Literature Today, March 1, 2007

In the past few years, many excellent films have been adapted from equally excellent graphic novels—for instance, Max Collins's *Road to Perdition*, John Wagner and Vince Locke's *A History of Violence*, Alan Moore and David Lloyd's *V for Vendetta*, Frank Miller's *Sin City*, and Daniel Clowes's *Art School Confidential*. Several more films made from graphic novels—including an adaptation of Frank Miller and Lynn Varley's retelling of the Greeks' stand against the Persians at Thermopylae, entitled *300*—are also on the way. Yet another graphic novel, Art Spiegelman's *Maus*, has won the Pulitzer Prize and was the subject of an exhibition at the Museum of Modern Art in New York. Alan Moore and Dave Gibbons's *Watchmen* has achieved cult status on university campuses. Is this recent popularity of the graphic novel in Hollywood, with prize and museum committees, on campuses and, it must be added, in chain bookstores, an instant trend that will soon pass, or does it point to a deeper, more lasting shift in our culture? My fifteen years of teaching this new genre at the university level have provided some hints of an answer to this question. The excitement of newness alone is not very lasting in academe, as elsewhere. But instead of sputtering out like other trendy fireworks, the graphic novel has been steadily gaining in brightness among audiences both inside and outside the academy. Why? My conclusions to date, which have not and probably will never pass the test of scientific scrutiny, but which seem sensible to me, follow.

First, it seems to me that the graphic novel represents the answer of the book—and people who love to read and make books—to the challenge of the electronic screen, including film, television, the Internet, and video games. Just as the theater's survival was challenged by the rise of film, which led playwrights and theater crews to create new techniques and special effects, so traditional literature and the book medium in which it exists have found a way to combine their strengths with that of painting, another threatened medium in the electronic age, and to meet the screen on its largely visual ground while retaining the pleasures and advantages of

* From the March-April 2007 issue of *World Literature Today* (81:2), pages 24-28. Copyright 2007 *World Literature Today*.

the book. Literary books can offer depth, subtlety, privacy, and intimacy. They also offer an experience controlled by the reader, who can open and close a book at any time, unlike the film or TV viewer, who must follow a film or television show more or less continuously while it is being screened and finds interruptions a disservice. Yet the advantages of the electronic media are many: presentations in the electronic media are relatively concise and offer speed of apprehension, are relatively easy on the eyes compared to print (except for some badly illuminated computer screens), include sound, and can portray such things as subtle facial expressions and landscapes better than literature can. In the form of video games, they also offer interactivity. Whereas the graphic novel cannot include sound, it provides many of the advantages of both print and electronic media while creating a unique and subtle experience all its own (including strikingly lettered indications of sound). Whether we're dealing with *Watchmen* (known as the *Ulysses* of the graphic novel for its subtlety, stylistic variety, philosophical reach, and depth of characterization, and which is much more approachable than Joyce's *Ulysses*) or Marjane Satrapi's *Persepolis*—a stark and harrowing look into what it was like to grow up under the Shah of Iran and then Khomeini—the graphic novel gives us the subtlety and intimacy we get from good literary books while providing the speed of apprehension and the excitingly scrambled, hybrid reading experience we get from watching, say, computer screens that are full of visuals as well as text.

The graphic novel also provides something else, as Marshall McLuhan noted long ago and Scott McCloud has since reiterated: imaginative interactivity. Comics for McCloud constitute a Zen-like "invisible art," which makes use of the blank spaces, or gutters, that exist between panels and which are the very definition of the unique comics experience. According to McCloud, the reader must fill in these blanks, thus imagining a good deal of the action that takes place in comics. It follows that the mental interactivity of the reader with a graphic novel is much more pronounced and essential than that which occurs when he or she watches a film or high-definition television, in which there are ordinarily no blank spaces for a reader to fill in imaginatively. Thus, the graphic novel routinely manages to provide a powerful interactive experience that has something in common with the interactivity of even that most interactive genre of all, the video game.

It is auspicious, indeed, for those who value books and reading that the book has managed to offer this new, hybrid form of reading that combines visual with verbal rhetoric, for the screen is a very powerful competitor—seeming to threaten, at times, the erasure of reading altogether, except perhaps among those people (usually of an older generation) most devoted to it. Even people like myself, who value traditional reading enormously, often find it more appealing to surf the unique blend of text and picture that is the Internet rather than to read a book when suffering a spell of insomnia. Video games are hypnotic, to judge from the scores of young people playing them devotedly in shopping malls. Television is actually addictive, as several studies have shown. Films provide a great Friday-night social experience. Therefore, it is no wonder that, owing to the impact of these various visual media, from year to year students display less and less patience with unillustrated texts, especially long ones; teaching *Moby Dick* or *Paradise Lost* is now a job that takes far more persistence, devotion, and flair to perform successfully than was the case in the past. Even with the best teachers, many students cannot now rise to the challenge of reading pure texts. Because of the influence of the electronic screen, that form of reading is slowly being lost, except for a few specialist readers, much like the amateur playing of classical piano, which is now a vanishing art. The new hybrid visual and verbal reading—different from traditional reading but fortunately no less subtle, intelligent, or, in its way, demanding—is rapidly taking its place. That is why, I believe, English departments—rather than art or communications departments—are leading the movement into the teaching and study of the graphic novel. English departments are book-oriented, students are reading pure text much less than they used to, and English departments are trying to find a way to react to this trend in order to ensure their own survival.

It is only honest to admit that even the most motivated readers, whether they are twenty-five or sixty-five, can become physically exhausted when reading pure text in books and staring at those little black marks on white paper for long periods with no visual relief. A long, unillustrated text takes a long time to read, and many people don't quite have the stamina or, more importantly, the taste for that anymore. They just don't want to put in the time, no matter how fascinating the book. They wonder why the writer could not have been more concise. They want a quick read rather than a thick text, not because they are unintelligent or lazy, but simply because they are used to quick electronic perception. Also, despite all of the clichés written about purely textual novels allowing us to imagine characters and places, the truth is that most of us who are not visual artists cannot really visualize what a writer is talking about when he or she describes a person or physical object; most of us need to see that person or object, and television and films—and graphic novels—allow us to do just that. (The fact that graphic novels are so easily adaptable to other visual media also partially explains why so many talented artists and writers are drawn to the genre these days.)

At the same time, books as a medium are not going away, just as theater survived films. I—and apparently a lot of other people—like to go to bookstores, to hold books, to flip through them, and even to read them while drinking some coffee. There is something special—call it privacy and intimacy—between ourselves and a book that we are not ready to give up. And then there's the fact that books don't black out on us sometimes, as electronic devices do. The graphic novel is the ideal evolution of the book in its attempt to adapt to the new electronic age. I do not mean to imply that text-based books will disappear in the foreseeable future, and even *Watchmen* includes a substantial piece of pure (and brilliantly written) text at the end of each chapter. Nor do I think that English departments are going to stop teaching Melville or Milton in their original, textual versions anytime soon (although there exist terrific graphic-novel adaptations of Eliot's *Waste Land* by Martin Rowson and of Kafka's "Metamorphosis" by Peter Kuper). I think text-based books will exist for a long time to come, but I also think that the balance between purely textual books and graphic novels in terms of numbers of readers will continue to shift in favor of graphic novels. I also predict that the graphic novel will continue to hold its own against the electronic screen and that, if handheld electronic book readers ever prove themselves (as they have so far failed to do), the graphic novel will be an extremely popular form of reading in that format as well.

While all this relates to the technical reason that the graphic novel is becoming prevalent today—namely, a diminution of our ability and desire to read straight text, while we retain our taste for the intimacy of the book and find a combination of text and picture very congenial—there is also one primary cultural reason for the emerging triumph of the graphic novel. It is the reason comics were and still are considered childish by many people. In a child's imagination, the line between the physically possible and the physically impossible is blurred, as it is in comics, where a man can leap tall buildings in a single bound and creatures may metamorphose into other creatures at will. It is very easy for the artist to make the move from the realistic to the fantastic and vice versa in comics; it can be done from one panel to the next or even within one panel. We accept strange transformations in comics; that is perhaps the very essence of the cultural side of the comics experience, running from Lyonel Feininger's *Wee Willie Winkie's World* to Shuster and Siegel's *Superman* and beyond. (That is why we are able to accept Peter Kuper's superb rendering of Kafka's bug/human character, Gregor Samsa, in Kuper's adaptation of "The Metamorphosis," so readily.) In short, I feel that the cultural reason that serious comics seem to appeal to so many readers today is that we are living in a world in which our reality might instantly prove, and often does prove, to be completely different from what we thought it was.

I happened to be teaching Alan Moore and David Lloyd's *V for Vendetta*, which ends with the Houses of Parliament being blown up, at the University of Oklahoma around the time when the Alfred P. Murrah building was destroyed by a truck bomb about fifteen miles north of my classroom. I remember the class and I remarking that we were now living in a comic-book world. And many of us have been teaching *Watchmen*, which details a catastrophic attack on New York City, before and since 9/11. Again, we are living in a comic-book world—that is, a world that seems to partake of the elastic landscape of a comic book, so ready to explode from mundane realism into a fantastic shape in a second. Moore and Gibbons, who created *Watchmen* as a serial in 1987–88, prove that verbal and visual poets can indeed be seers, as the Romans believed. (And in a particularly brilliant observation based on William Burroughs's "cut-up" collage technique, Moore shamanistically implies in chapter 11 that, for the reader, the panels and gutters of *Watchmen* itself are comparable to the multiple television screens that Veidt watches simultaneously in order to discern the shape of the future, thus turning the reader into a seer as well.)

The world has caught up with Moore and Gibbons and has become as outlandish as the virtual world they describe. Moore's fantastic plot in *Watchmen*, in particular, and its elastic rendering in comics seem to duplicate our own explosive experience better than any other medium does. No wonder Art Spiegelman found it so possible to render his personal 9/11 experience in a graphic novel, *In the Shadow of No Towers*, or that Sid Jacobson and Ernie Colón have just turned the 9/11 commission report into a graphic novel, *The Illustrated 9/11 Commission Report*. The elasticity of comics makes Jacobson and Colón's adaptation more apt, more suited to our sense of how "unreal" the Twin Towers events were, than the 9/11 report itself. And their adaptation has a diagrammatic quality that makes these fantastic events easier to read about and to understand than might be possible in prose alone. A comic-book-like incident, planes deliberately flying into the Twin Towers, has actually become a comic book. The new comic book makes 9/11 no more or less "real" than it was; it just fits those events naturally, or so it seems.

But the comic-book novel is of our times not only because many of today's events are truly "fantastic"—that is, horrific and unexpected. The elasticity of the comic-book novel also allows it to bring out the fantastic element inherent—but not often noticed—in mundane reality. One of my (and many of my students') favorite graphic novels is Raymond Briggs's *Ethel and Ernest*. Briggs is one of the premier contemporary British illustrated children's book creators. His *Father Christmas* and *The Snowman* have sold many, many copies to parents eager to show and tell these illustrated stories to their children. *Ethel and Ernest* is a serious, subtle, and gentle biography of his parents and also an account of British history from circa 1930 (when they were married) to 1971, the year in which both died. We watch as Ethel and Ernest move through a life made difficult by the Depression and the Blitz and then made incomprehensible to them by rapid social change after World War II. Despite this seriousness of subject and purpose, however, the characters are rendered in gentle, slightly blurred and dreamy colors. The prose is simple, relatively sparse, and limited to dialogue. The word balloons swell from small, smooth, and regular to jagged, large, and full of emphasis. The world of Ethel and Ernest, rendered nostalgically by their son despite its many difficulties, becomes a fairy-tale landscape inhabited by a noble (if sometimes silly and ignorant) queen and king, although Briggs never directly refers to his parents as such. He has taken his and his parents' mundane and sometimes not-so-mundane reality and brought out all of its inherent magic, thus collapsing the boundary between reality and fantasy. In short, Briggs's book is really a children's book for adults, and his intention seems to be to comfort us, just as children are comforted by a gently told tale.

Whether it deals primarily with fantasy or with reality, the graphic novel is a form suited to the contemporary age because of its appeal to our newly learned sense that reality can very quickly become fantasy, and vice versa, as well as its unique and comforting combination of the qualities of both book and screen. If we add the enormous popularity of Japanese manga with American preteens, as well as the remembered comfort inherent in the illustrated children's books with which we are all familiar, to the present impetus toward reading sophisticated comics, I contend that the graphic novel will continue to displace (if never completely replace) purely textual writing and that it will eventually become the most popular form of reading. That is because I think that, fortunately or unfortunately, we will watch reality and fantasy morph into each other many, many times in our collective lives in the years to come, not always pleasantly. The good news is that the graphic novel now offers just as many fine creative talents—and as subtle, plastic, and wonderful a reading experience—as any literary genre ever has done.

STEPHEN E. TABACHNICK *is chair of the English department at the University of Memphis and the author, most recently, of* Fiercer than Tigers: The Life and Works of Rex Warner *(2002) and* Lawrence of Arabia: An Encyclopedia *(2004). He is currently editing* Approaches to Teaching the Graphic Novel, *a collection of original essays, for the Modern Language Association.*

2

Out of the "Comics Ghetto":
Graphic Novels as Serious Literature

Editor's Introduction

When Art Spiegelman's *Maus* won a Pulitzer Prize in 1992, it confirmed what many had long believed: Graphic novels can be great literature. By the following decade, graphic novels had finally started gaining widespread recognition, and in 2005, *Time* named Alan Moore's *Watchmen* to its list of the best 100 English-language novels since 1923. The following year, Alison Bechdel's graphic-novel memoir *Fun Home* made many publications' year-end best-of lists, earning a "best comic book" nod from *Publishers Weekly* and topping *Time*'s "10 Best Books" list.

Critics aren't the only ones championing graphic novels. In 2007, Gene Luen Yang's *American Born Chinese* was nominated for a National Book Award in the young people's literature category, and it won the Michael L. Printz Award for teen literature, given by the Young Adult Library Services Association (YALSA) of the American Library Association (ALA). David Small's *Stitches* was also nominated for the National Book Award in 2009 for the young people's literature category, and in 2010, Geoffrey Hayes won the Theodor Seuss Geisel Award for most distinguished work for beginning readers published in the United States, given by ALA's Association for Library Services to Children (ALSC).

The articles in this chapter center on graphic novels' recent surge in respectability. In "Graphic Novels are Legit Lit," the first selection, Micah Mertes highlights the work of Richard Graham, a computer-science and visual-literacy liaison for the University of Nebraska-Lincoln. Graham has focused his research on graphic novels, which he insists are "flexing their literary muscle."

In the following piece, "Comics No Longer a Joke in Academia," Lisa Cornwell discusses college and university courses devoted to comics. While scattershot courses for aspiring artists still outnumber dedicated programs of study, more courses are being offered all the time, and demand for them is increasing. At the same time, many college English departments are beginning to study graphic novels as literature, despite what some students describe as a lingering "academic prejudice" against the medium.

In "From Pulp to Pulitzer: How the Underground Comic Found Its Way to the Mainstream," Fritz Lanham interviews Gene Kannenberg, Jr., an assistant professor of English at the University of Houston-Downtown, and profiles Marjane Satrapi, author of *Persepolis*, a graphic memoir some critics rank alongside *Maus* and *Watchmen*.

In "The Plot Thickens . . . ", the subsequent piece in this chapter, Linda Lou further explores college comics courses and interviews Rocco Versaci, author of *This Book Contains Graphic Language: Comics as Literature*, an attempt to "discuss and portray comics in a way many people have not analyzed or considered," according to Lou. Versaci teaches a class called "Comics as Literature" at California's Palomar College, and in explaining to Lou why he's so drawn to graphic novels, he says they "create meaning that's unavailable to forms like film and prose."

Chris Mautner next looks at how teachers and librarians are making educational use of graphic novels in "Once-Avoided Comics Welcomed in Schools." David Ball, a professor at Dickinson College, tells Mautner graphic novels can help students develop critical and analytical thinking skills applicable in the real world.

In the final piece, "The Big Battle," Peter Rowe considers why some artists and industry pundits are suspicious of mainstream acceptance and would prefer comics to retain their grit and "air of disrepute," as writer Tom Spurgeon of *The Comics Reporter* puts it. An accompanying "Graphic Novel Starter Kit" sidebar lists the ten selections Rowe feels every comics newcomer should read.

Graphic Novels Are Legit Lit[*]

By Micah Mertes
Lincoln Journal Star, March 1, 2009

"Watchmen" hits theaters this week, an adaptation of arguably the most influential graphic novel, well, ever.

You've likely watched the trailer by now, but you might not know anything about the source material.

So . . .

The 1986 book by Alan Moore was one of the first of its kind to land in the hands of mainstream readers. And it helped launch a whole new kind of storytelling: comic books for grown-ups.

This was not the funny papers, not silly kids fodder.

Despite its bright colors, speech clouds and masked heroes, "Watchmen" proved that a graphic novel can be as complex and sophisticated as any genre.

And since "Watchmen," each subsequent graphic novel masterwork has crystallized the medium's place in legit lit. Not just as "literary fiction's half-wit cousin," as writer Dave Eggers said, "but, more accurately, the mutant sister who can do everything fiction can."

"They're literature, sure, and memoir and biography and journalism," said Richard Graham, computer science and visual literacy liaison for the University of Nebraska-Lincoln libraries digital media program. "All sorts of people are interested in comics now, especially in the field of education."

About five years back, Graham made comic books and graphic novels his research focus, in turn beefing up Love Library's collection of the genre. The criteria for each entry was always: Does it have academic value? This hasn't been too tough a sell.

"My father still shakes his head at an academic who studies 'funny books,'" Graham said. He "questions its value. There is still some of that old guard or anach-

---

ronistic thinking. A lot of people are quick to dismiss them. But they're growing more accepted in all the rank and file.

"They're flexing their literary muscle."

Consider the 1992 Pulitzer Prize-winning book "Maus," which chronicles the true story of a family of Holocaust survivors and their children. The book is a dead-serious account, despite the fact that the characters are illustrated as cartooney mice, cats and pigs instead of Jews, Nazis and Poles. The book is used in a handful of English classes at UNL, including American Jewish Fiction.

" 'Maus' was the biggest factor in legitimizing the graphic novel," said Bob Hall, local comic artist. "It sort of pulled the idea of graphic novels into the main-stream."

The "big, wonderful thing" about graphic novels, Hall said, is that they've also managed to escape the caped confines of the superhero genre. And even when they do explore it, it's done so in a manner that's cynical of simple heroism. You won't find much "rah-rah" derring-do in "Watchmen" or Frank Miller's "The Dark Knight Returns."

"The very refreshing way in which they explored a superhero world," Hall said, "had a big influence on the writing of superhero comics thereafter."

And on the selling of superhero comics.

The production and sales of the individual monthly comic books has dwindled in the past few decades, due in part to the fact that issues get packaged into thick paperback compendiums.

"In the old days," said Larry Lorenz, owner of Trade-A-Tape Comic Center, "they didn't want to have things that would last more than one issue. Now, every-thing is like a six- or seven-part story, at least. They may eventually do away with the individual comics altogether."

Which would likely continue to break whatever barrier remains between books and comic books.

Perhaps then that awful term "the funny papers" will at long last die the horrible death it's always deserved.

SURVIVAL GUIDE

It's never too late to jump into the world of comics.
Here's a survival guide to get you on your way.

COMIC BOOKS VS. GRAPHIC NOVELS

Graphic novels are unlike comic books in that they're self-contained. They have a beginning, middle and end.

They typically forgo caped crusader capers in favor of weightier topics and bleaker tales. Artist Eddie Campbell said the graphic novel's goal is "to take the form of the comic book, which has become an embarrassment, and raise it to a more ambitious and meaningful level, forging a whole new art."

When did they emerge?

Opinions on the origin of the graphic novel vary. But it's generally agreed that the form popped up in the last quarter of the 20th century.

Most consider the birth of the graphic novel to be 1978 with the release of Will Eisner's "A Contract with God." However, the term was coined in 1964 by comics critic Richard Kyle.

HOW TO READ THEM

Comics used to carry a pretty nasty stigma, so you might not have grown up reading them. You might be—gasp!—"comics illiterate."

Here are a couple of things to keep in mind while reading:

1. Don't go too fast. Graphic novels don't take that long to read, but the author and artist (if they're good) have packed those frames with subtle information that you might not spot with a quick scan.
2. Savor the language. Because there are relatively so few words in a graphic novel, the writer is forced to be more precise in the dialogue and descriptions. And it (usually) makes for great writing.
3. Don't dismiss the genre after one bad book. "Persepolis" author Marjane Satrapi advises: "Like anything new, you have to cultivate your interest."
4. Don't be embarrassed about reading a graphic novel. This is a relatively new, exciting, and, yes, respectable genre. Trix might just be for kids, but comic books are for everybody.

Comics No Longer a Joke in Academia[*]

By Lisa Cornwell
The Associated Press, December 29, 2007

As a fine-arts graduate student in the early 1980s, Carol Tyler thought she should hide her interest in cartoon drawing from teachers: An art form associated with comic books and comic strips wasn't considered college material.

Last year, as a professional cartoonist and graphic novelist, Tyler taught the first University of Cincinnati class in comics art.

Other colleges have also started such classes amid growing critical and academic respect for comics.

Courses begun in 2005 at the University of Alaska Fairbanks, for example, are drawing professional artists and public-school teachers.

Applications have increased by at least 50 percent at the Center for Cartoon Studies in White River Junction, Vt.—which was founded two years ago and won state approval this year for a master's degree in fine arts.

"Schools are now recognizing the creative and commercial value of comics," Tyler said as she watched students outline their pencil drawings in ink.

"An interest in comics and cartooning doesn't have to be a secret anymore."

Not only artists are interested in comics at the academic level.

A course at Ohio State University on the history of cartooning in American newspapers is offered regularly. Other classes there include one on the graphic novel and another on comic text.

The medium is slowly being accepted by academia—thanks in large part to the growing quality of graphic novels, memoirs, histories and journalism, said Jared Gardner, an associate professor of English and film at OSU.

Since the late 1990s, he said, some of the best works of American literature have been produced in comic form.

"It is most definitely the case that the quality and accomplishments of the work have overcome the ingrained cultural conservatism of many academics," he said by e-mail.

OSU ranks among the friendliest places in the nation for comics study, Gardner said, because of the Cartoon Research Library and the triennial Festival of Cartoon Art, next planned for 2010.

"But even outside Ohio State," he said, "the climate is improving every year."

Some of Tyler's students hope to learn skills useful for careers in advertising, film, video-game design or illustration. Some just enjoy comics; others want to produce comics or graphic novels.

"I started drawing comics when I was about 12 but had sort of put it aside," said Mariana Young, a 25-year-old who wants to become a professional cartoonist and produce a one-character series to be published quarterly.

Tyler's students learn graphic design, composition, lettering, layout and how to draw figures that convey emotion. She also tries to show them how to organize their thoughts to deliver clear and concise ideas. Story lines have included the effect of nannies on a student's life and recollections of a colorful grandfather.

Ben Towle, director of the National Association of Comic Art Educators, said it's too soon to have hard data on numbers or where new classes are being taught. But the association is fielding many more inquiries about starting classes.

"There are a lot of scattershot courses as opposed to dedicated programs," he said, "but you wouldn't even have seen that five years ago."

Demand is also growing for established courses, and some schools have waiting lists.

The number of freshmen in the cartooning major at the School of Visual Arts in New York more than doubled from 2002 to last year. The Savannah (Ga.) College of Art and Design offered comics art in 1992 as an elective to a handful of students. The school now has almost 300 undergraduates and 50 graduate students pursuing bachelor's and master's degrees in sequential art, also known as comics art.

Much of the credit goes to the emergence in the 1980s of graphic novels offering more complex and complete story lines for more mature audiences. They typically are more durably bound and longer than the floppy comic magazines that told the tales of Superman or the antics of small-town teenager Archie Andrews and friends.

The graphic novel's increased critical acclaim and greater visibility in mainstream bookstores and libraries have contributed to the growing respect for comics art. Educators also cite the worldwide popularity and influence of Japanese comics known as *manga*—written for children and adults—and the transformation of graphic novels such as *Ghost World* into Hollywood films.

More schools are also studying comics as literature or creative writing in English departments. And although art educators and students say academic prejudice still exists, there are more academic conferences on comics, and libraries are increasingly carrying comic works.

"With graphic novels and *manga*, librarians have seen an upsurge in demand the last three to five years, and many say *manga* is their highest circulation material," said Ann Kim, editor of special projects and graphic novels for *Library Journal*. "There is definitely more respect now."

From Pulp to Pulitzer[*]

How the Underground Comic Found Its Way to the Mainstream

By Fritz Lanham
Houston Chronicle, August 29, 2004

Art Spiegelman's Maus I and II, about his Jewish father's experiences in the Holocaust, won a special Pulitzer Prize in 1992 and made it OK for people who normally carry around Anna Karenina to be seen reading a book of mostly pictures. Pictures of mice and cats, incidentally.

The two-volume Maus is among the most admired examples of the "graphic novel," a slight misnomer since many of the best-known specimens—the books of Robert Crumb and Harvey Pekar, and more recently Marjane Satrapi—are autobiography rather than fiction.

Sept. 7 brings Spiegelman's meditation on Sept. 11, In the Shadow of No Towers. This week marks the publication of Satrapi's Persepolis 2, sequel to last year's widely praised Persepolis: The Story of a Girlhood, about growing up in Ayatollah Khomeini's Iran. The near-simultaneous arrival of these two important books invites a look at the emerging art form. For years these books have been seeping out of the comic-book ghetto and into the mainstream, and now the current seems to be picking up speed.

Look, for example, at the catalog of Pantheon, a big-name imprint that's part of the Random House empire, and count the number of graphic novels—more than 15, Spiegelman's and Satrapi's among them. Go into Brazos Bookstore and note that owner Karl Kilian, a longtime and careful observer of the public's book-buying habits, has installed a large, freestanding display devoted to comics and graphic novels.

Finally, pick up the July 7 issue of the New York Times magazine. In a 7,000-word cover story Charles McGrath, former editor of the Times Book Review, opines that graphic novels may someday replace traditional novels as the popular literary form, just as the latter replaced poetry in the 19th century.

ANATOMY OF A GRAPHIC NOVEL

So what, exactly, is a graphic novel, and how does it differ from the humble comic book?

Gene Kannenberg Jr., an assistant professor of English at University of Houston-Downtown, teaches comics as a literary form. He is not fond of the term graphic novel but has come to accept it. It really means nothing more than "a book by a cartoonist that has a spine rather than being stapled," he says. In other words, a very fat comic book. Spiegelman famously said with Maus he wanted to do a comic book that would require use of a bookmark.

Will Eisner's A Contract With God, published in 1978, was the first to call itself a graphic novel, although the phrase already had currency among comics aficionados. Eisner wanted to tell stories for adults, and the graphic-novel moniker, plus the fat, booklike look of the thing, were ways to convey that ambition.

The so-called underground comics movement of the late 1960s and early 1970s was a major taproot of the contemporary graphic novel. Crumb is the name always mentioned but, Kannenberg says, there were many others contributing comics to alternative newspapers like the East Village Other and the Rag in Austin and later collecting them into books.

In many cases, he says, these were people who grew up on the irreverent humor of Mad magazine. Mix Mad with the anarchic spirit of the counterculture and you get artists who "realize comics are words and pictures you can do anything with," Kannenberg says.

"You don't have to work for Archie or Superman. You can do whatever you want. And that whatever you want has blossomed, finally, into a wide variety of stuff."

The mid-1980s brought milestone graphic novels that raised the profile of the genre among general readers. The big three, according to Kannenberg, were Maus I, Frank Miller's Batman: The Dark Knight Returns (a reconception of the familiar character as an aging, inner-demon-driven caped crusader), and Alan Moore and Dave Gibbons' Watchmen, an intricately plotted deconstructive take on superheroes.

But there wasn't yet that critical mass of important work in book form that would make graphic novels a staple of traditional bookstores as well as comic-book shops. That has come more recently, fueled in part by Hollywood's discovery of the genre (Ghost World was based on a Dan Clowes graphic novel), by the decision of mainstream publishers such as Pantheon to jump in with both feet and by the willingness of influential publications like the New York Times Book Review to review graphic novels as serious literature.

WHO ARE THE READERS?

The audience skews young—people in their 20s and 30s—and male, Kannenberg says, though some of the Japanese comics, or manga, have drawn young female readers into the fold.

Yet you don't have to look far to find graphic novels that will appeal to their parents as well. For admirers of high literature, there's Peter Kuper's chilling version of Kafka's Metamorphosis. Kuper's black-and-white, woodcut-like illustrations convey the nightmare quality (though not the absurdist humor) of the original. Martin Rowson's febrile technique invests Tristram Shandy, that rollicking 18th-century masterpiece, with 21st-century comic energy.

Both of those are illustrated versions of pre-existing literary works. Arguably the more "pure" graphic novels are those with art and text by the same person. One superb recent example is Chris Ware's Jimmy Corrigan: The Smartest Kid on Earth, a touching, psychologically complex story of the sad-sack 36-year-old title character and his reunion with the father who abandoned him years before. The pace is leisurely, the color palate subtle, the tone plaintive and elegiac. Published in 2000, Jimmy Corrigan is definitely a book for grown-ups.

As are Satrapi's Persepolis books. Born in 1970, Satrapi grew up the daughter of educated, secular, liberal-minded parents. Smart and spirited, she bucks against her repressive, mullah-ridden society yet can't escape loneliness and alienation in Europe, where she attends boarding school. Simple, flat, black-and-white drawings record the physical and emotional oscillations of her coming of age.

Although Satrapi trained as an artist, she also likes to write, so "for me the form of the graphic novel was absolutely obvious," she said in a phone interview from Paris, where she lives today.

Armed with a basic scenario in her head she produces the text and the images at the same time, she says. "There's nothing absolutely systematic about it."

Asked about influences, she cites everything from Italian neo-realist movies to the Argentinian cartoonist Jose Muñoz to the woodblock prints of Swiss artist Felix Vallotton. Movies showed her how small anecdotes—a poor man gets his bicycle stolen, say—can be teased into a work exploring larger social themes.

She grew captivated by the possibilities of black and white. "You cannot cheat when you make (an artwork) in black and white," she says. "You make a lousy drawing, you put some color on it, and it looks nice. With black and white, if it's lousy everyone will see it."

Judging from those she meets at her signings, most of her readers aren't comic-book buffs but people whose normal fare is the traditional novel, she says. "Which is a very good thing. It means people who aren't used to this form of expression are getting interested." She agrees that the American audience for graphic novels is growing rapidly—in Europe such books have long been respectable.

Satrapi is currently at work on the screenplay of an animated version of Persepolis, which she will direct. Sadly, her books cannot be published in Iran, but English-language copies apparently are circulating surreptitiously, she says.

HOW THE GRAPHIC NOVEL STACKS UP

How good are the best graphic novels? As good as anything produced by traditional writers or filmmakers or painters, says Kannenberg. The fact is, most novels, most movies, most cultural products of every sort are mediocre or worse, and the bad-to-good ratio may even be a little higher in comics. But a handful in every medium are good—even great.

"I don't think there's much that film can't do," he says. "I don't think there's much that prose can't do, I don't think there's much that poetry can't do. Comics are exactly the same. I think what limits comics are the preconceptions—sometimes of the people producing them, but also of the larger public."

Kannenberg doesn't buy McGrath's theory that graphic novels may someday replace the traditional novel. Brazos Bookstore's Karl Kilian doesn't buy it either.

Kilian, however, does see "one of those cultural shifts going on right now." What drove that home to him, he says, was coming across a volume on Robert Crumb in the University Press of Mississippi's conversations with artists and writers series, which includes such high-culture stalwarts as Susan Sontag and I.B. Singer.

Previously Kilian had shelved graphic novels in various parts of his store—some in history, others in fiction. Since he's brought them together on one display he's sold about a hundred books, he says. He couldn't immediately compare numbers but says that amounts to "a lot more" than a year ago. The unquestionable quality of a handful of graphic novels—Maus and Ben Katchor's Julius Knipl, Real Estate Photographer are Kilian's examples—have elevated the genre as a whole in readers eyes, he says.

So expect to see more graphic novels on your own and your friends' bookshelves. Whether wider acceptance will be a good or a bad thing for the medium is perhaps a question. As comics historian Roger Sabin has noted, lots of those who create and consume comics come from the social margins—and actually like it there.

WORKS CITED

The Metamorphosis. By Franz Kafka, adapted by Peter Kuper. Crown, $18.

Jimmy Corrigan: The Smartest Kid on Earth. By Chris Ware. Pantheon. $17.95.

The Boulevard of Broken Dreams. By Kim Deitch with Simon Deitch. Pantheon, $21.

The Plot Thickens . . . *

More Colleges Are Turning to Graphic Novels and Comics as Legitimate Literary Forms, Teaching Tools

By Linda Lou
San Diego Union-Tribune, March 23, 2008

When most people think about comics, their views are limited to newspaper funnies or thin, sometimes juvenile tales of superhero adventures.

But experts, including Palomar College professor Rocco Versaci, say comic books and graphic novels that are sophisticated, emotionally gripping and deal with complex subjects have been emerging over the past 20 years or so.

Still, some people don't know that award-winning titles such as "Maus," "Persepolis" and "Fun Home" even exist.

Times are changing, however, and students are increasingly studying graphic novels in classrooms, said Nancy Frey, an associate professor of literacy who works with teachers and aspiring teachers at San Diego State University.

Frey and others such as Versaci are part of a growing number of educators encouraging readers to see comics as a legitimate literary form.

Versaci had a book on the subject published this year. "This Book Contains Graphic Language: Comics as Literature" presents comics as a literary form with comparisons to genres such as memoirs, new journalism, war films from the 1940s and 1950s, and "real" literature.

Many examples highlighted in the book, Versaci's first, are independent or alternative comics. Versaci, 40, said he wanted to discuss and portray comics in a way that many people have not analyzed or considered.

This fall, Versaci will teach a class on the subject, called "Comics as Literature," at Palomar College.

SERIOUS SUBJECTS

A wider acceptance of comics began in the late 1980s after three works—"Maus," "Watchmen" and "Batman: The Dark Knight Returns"—were printed, Versaci said.

Art Spiegelman's "Maus" is a graphic novel about the experiences of Spiegelman's father as a Holocaust survivor in which Jews are depicted as humans with mouse faces and Nazis as people with faces of cats. "Watchmen" is a sophisticated comic series about superheroes, Versaci said. After Spiegelman's "Maus II," published in 1991, won a special Pulitzer Prize in 1992, graphic novels gained even more legitimacy, Frey said.

"Maus," published in 1986, became a model and inspired later works that focus on storytelling and experiment with the visual format, said Christian Hill, an assistant professor of sequential art and illustration at California State University Fullerton.

As a result, works have become more meaningful, Hill said. In turn, graphic novels have become more respectable, he said. Hill's students are already familiar with them and manga, or Japanese comics.

But it doesn't mean that the prejudice against graphic novels has been eliminated.

Despite the growing acceptance of graphic novels and comics, some teachers still would rather students read "Pride and Prejudice" than "Persepolis," although both works question the role of women in society, Frey said.

"Persepolis," by Marjane Satrapi, tells tales of an outspoken girl growing up in Iran during the Islamic revolution. The animated film adaptation of "Persepolis" was nominated for an Academy Award this year.

Even the term "graphic novel" is an example of a struggle for acceptance, Hill and Versaci said.

Technically, a comic book is a single issue that is part of a series. Graphic novels can be a collection of a series of comics or one complete story.

Acceptance is also about perception. Hill said graphic novel sounds more prestigious than comics even though both are part of the same art form.

'UNIQUE' COMMUNICATION

As a boy, Versaci devoured comics about superheroes but later moved onto other reading material. His interest in comics returned after hearing Spiegelman talk at Indiana University, where Versaci was working on a doctorate in English literature.

Versaci said he enjoys books and movies, but there is something special about blending words and images.

"They are able to create meaning that's unavailable to forms like film and prose," he said. "Comics communicate in a unique way."

The comics form, Versaci said, makes it obvious to readers that they are getting an interpretation of the author's thoughts, not the absolute truth.

The visual techniques add a different layer to the story, Frey said, with the use of color, lines and shapes.

"It taps into another level of consciousness and understanding," she said.

Anna Joy Springer, an assistant professor of literature at University of California San Diego, said graphic novels work well for teaching about structure and style.

Some are examined in architectural classes, she said, such as "Jimmy Corrigan: The Smartest Kids on Earth" by Chris Ware and "Understanding Comics: The Invisible Art" by Scott McCloud.

Ware's work includes illustrations of Chicago landscapes and buildings and images of Chicago World's Fair of 1893.

VISUAL WORLD

At Palomar College, the selection of comics at the campus library is growing in part because they are being used as teaching material in classes, officials said.

Versaci said comics invite students to think more broadly about literature and get them to talk in class.

"Some students respond more deeply to the graphic novel because of the visual world they live in," said Andrea Bell, an English professor at Palomar.

Nicholas Ivins, 26, a former student, said he used to think of literature in terms of "The Great Gatsby" or other older titles, until he discovered alternative and independent comics through Versaci's class.

Ivins, a graphic designer, said class discussions focused on analyzing plot, art, themes and storytelling techniques, like other literature classes.

At Versaci's recent book signing in Mission Valley, about a dozen people stopped by to chat. Some didn't know much about comics, but even regular comics readers like Mark Leo, 23, had not heard of titles such as "Maus."

Leo, a University of California Santa Barbara graduate, said he wants to introduce graphic novels to an after-school reading club at the East Mesa Juvenile Detention Facility where he works as an office clerk. His co-workers, he said, don't buy his point of view.

"They just think I'm crazy," Leo said.

Some of Versaci's colleagues who don't usually read comics said they are using them as teaching material, including "Maus" and "Fun Home," a graphic novel-memoir about sexuality, psychology and family that was nominated for a National Book Critics Circle Award.

Abbie Cory is using "Fun Home" in her Women and Literature class this semester and will use "V for Vendetta" in her British novels class this fall. Cory said a friend who teaches at San Jose State University recommended it.

Graphic novels are on their way to being fully embraced, Cory said. "The novel has changed over time and this is one of the latest evolutions."

Once-Avoided Comics Welcomed in Schools[*]

By Chris Mautner
The Patriot-News (Harrisburg, Pa.), March 9, 2008

Historical relevance. Artistic self-awareness. Aesthetic beauty. Intertextuality. Epistemology.

These are the types of topics you might find students discussing in your average college English literature class.

The students in Dickinson College professor David Ball's class aren't dissecting Faulkner or Joyce, however, but comic books.

More specifically, they're dissecting the stories found in "McSweeney's Vol. 13," a Chris Ware-edited and highly acclaimed anthology of work by various alternative and independent cartoonists.

Welcome to "Graphic Narratives," a new course on "an emerging genre in contemporary American literature" as the syllabus states, that treats artists like Ware, Art Spiegelman ("Maus") and Alison Bechdel ("Fun Home") with the same level of inquiry that is normally reserved for Shakespeare and Hemingway.

"Some of the most exciting work that's been done in the last five years has been done in this interdisciplinary medium," Ball said. "My interest is both in the quality of the work itself, the way it's being produced, and in the way that it stretches your brain in different ways."

Ball's class is just one example of the many ways comics or "graphic novels" as they're called these days have infiltrated the academic world.

Long regarded even feared as a hindrance to literacy, comics are now seen not only as worthy of inclusion in college classrooms but also as an educational tool in K–12 classes and public libraries across the country.

The notion that comics might have educational value might be surprising to those whose knowledge of the medium is limited to the funny pages in their newspaper. But those who have labored in its trenches are well aware of its potential.

"If you're trying to use comics to educate someone or convey ideas, using pictures helps get information into the head very quickly," said Juniata College biology professor Jay Hosler, who moonlights as a cartoonist and has produced such acclaimed graphic novels as "Clan Apis" and "The Sandwalk Adventures."

Hosler, whose new book, "Optical Allusions" takes readers on a tour of how the human eye works, cites other things that comics do well, such as acting as an intermediate step to learning difficult concepts, or being able to control the rate at which you move through the story.

"What I've always found is that a lot of times educators are really excited about another tool," he said. "They're facing struggle on the ground and they know through experience they have to continually find . . . innovative ways to engage the student. That's the real challenge."

It's a tool that Scott Shaffer uses frequently. A reading teacher at Southeastern Middle School West in Fawn Grove, he recently formed an after-school comics club in which students learn how to make and eventually even print their own comic book stories.

"I tell the kids you don't have to be the best artist. We have kids coming in drawing stick figures," Shaffer said.

A longtime comics fan, Shaffer is well aware of the medium's educational potential.

"I could list for you a dozen reading skills that could be taught in isolation out of a comic book," he said, "such as making predictions . . . making inferences (between panels), . . . sequence of events, cause and effect, character, onomatopoeia really I use them not only in the club, but I also use them as a teaching tool in my own instruction in my classroom."

Public libraries have been adding graphic novels to their shelves to draw younger and wayward readers through their doors.

The public library in Elizabethtown, for example, recently held a "Teen Anime and Manga Night" (manga being the term for Japanese comics) that drew 31 attendees.

"If you've seen teenagers on the bus and they're reading anything, that's something a teen librarian is going to notice and want to have in their collection," said youth services librarian Mary Anne Stanley.

"There are certain specific customer groups who are primarily interested in that material who aren't necessarily drawn to novels of Jane Austen," she said. "Teenage boys and young men are often very happy to have graphic novels and comics available."

What's more, she added, comics "have some very challenging vocabulary and concepts even when you're talking about things that people don't ordinarily think of in that way, like superhero comics. You can get some pretty heady vocabulary out of that."

Comics can help a person become not only a better reader but a smarter one as well.

"I want students to become intelligent readers of a number of different manifestations of media, from Super Bowl ads to Shakespeare," Ball said. "The analytical and critical thinking skills that you apply to comics are ones that can be used when you're watching an ad of someone trying to sell you something, when you're reading a book of American literature. They are skills that are transferable."

The Big Battle[*]

It's Edge vs. Respectability as Graphic Novels Move into the Mainstream,
But Make No Mistake: The Art Form Retains Its Grit and Its Power

By Peter Rowe
San Diego Union-Tribune, July 22, 2007

Look, on the horizon! Is that a bird . . . a plane . . . or perhaps the final comics crisis? Is this armageddon for artists, Götterdämmerung for graphic novelists?

In the 20th century, comic books endured congressional hearings and parental condemnation. The industry, like Plastic Man, always bounced back. The 21st century, though, has ushered in a relentless new foe:

Respectability.

"We need some of that air of disrepute," said Tom Spurgeon, editor of The Comics Reporter, an online site. "I think that it retains a little bit of a cool factor that way."

Bad news, then. Graphic novels . . . essentially comic books that tell an extended narrative . . . continue to gain fans. Even among, alas, the cultural elite.

Still, graphic novels haven't totally sold out or abandoned their original fan base. At Comic-Con International this week, you won't be able to swing a Wookie costume without knocking over stacks of the stuff. They'll be all across the exhibit hall, every day. They'll be on panels: "The Many Faces of the Graphic Novel," noon Thursday. And they'll be taking home many of the Eisner Awards, when the industry honors its best and best-selling: 8:30–10:30 p.m. Friday.

But take a close look at two heavily-favored Eisner nominees, graphic novels both:

1. Alison Bechdel's "Fun Home" was a 2006 finalist for the National Book Critics Circle Award. *Time* dubbed it the best book of 2006. At *New York* magazine and *The Times of London*, it was listed among the year's 10 best books.

2. "American Born Chinese" by Gene Luen Yang was a National Book Award runner-up. It won the Michael L. Printz Award for Excellence in Young Adult Literature. From the American Library Association.

Let me repeat: The ALA. If librarians are applauding a book, how disreputable can it be?

Douglas Wolk, the author of "Reading Comics: How Graphic Novels Work and What They Mean" (Da Capo Press, $22.95), argues that some comic book fans cling to the outdated notion that they are rebels, immersed in an underground art form: "Nobody understands us! We're outcasts, we're the weird kids! Some day they'll understand!"

Wolk's rebuttal: "You know what? They understand."

Blame the graphic novel.

DRAWING THREE ACES

The trouble began 21 years ago. Between 1986 and '87, a trio of graphic novels carved deep cracks in the wall between comic books and mainstream culture.

"Batman: The Dark Knight Returns" was the first, and perhaps the least startling. All Frank Miller did was take the old tale of Bruce Wayne's alter ego, add despair and blend well. Miller's Batman is a graying warrior, and it's uncertain whether this superhero can stop crime—he can't even stop his ego-driven clashes with Superman.

"Dark Knight" was largely ignored outside the comic *cognoscenti*. Not so "Maus," published later in 1986. The first of two volumes, Art Spiegelman's work was revolutionary for its subject—one family's experience during and after the Holocaust, a harrowing account complete with murder, rape, suicide—and approach. Borrowing a page from George Orwell, Spiegelman transformed his characters into animals with human emotions.

In 1992, "Maus" won a special Pulitzer Prize.

That was the first and, to date, only graphic novel to ascend such official literary heights. But some argue "Maus" was followed by a greater work. In early 1987, "Watchmen" concluded its 12-issue run, delivering an epic murder mystery, Cold War melodrama and probing, skeptical examination of superhero-worship.

In 2005, when *Time* constructed a list of the 100 best English-language novels since 1923, Ayn Rand didn't make the cut. Neither did John Irving. But Alan Moore and Dave Gibbons did, for "Watchmen."

High culture's battlements had been breached. *The New Yorker* signaled this defeat by printing a cartoon of a man asking, "Now I have to pretend to like graphic novels, too?"

"Liking" is not required. Some, though, insist that awareness is.

"Anyone described as 'well read' would have to be at least familiar with a core sample of all the varieties of literature including poetry, essays, novels, short stories and nonfiction," said Andrew Arnold, *Time*'s comics critic from 2002 until early 2007. "So there should be no reason to exclude graphical literature as well.

"Exactly which books constitute the canon of graphical literature can be debated, but 'Watchmen' and 'Jimmy Corrigan' should certainly be on the list."

Oh my. This story was progressing so peacefully and then someone mentioned Chris Ware's "Jimmy Corrigan: The Smartest Kid on Earth." Those are—pow! sock! bam!—fightin' words.

AVALANCHE OF COVERAGE

During a recent telephone interview, Wolk pronounced himself ready to rumble. "I wanted to start some arguments," he said, explaining why he wrote "Reading Comics."

He's in luck, especially given his field. For starters, the whole "graphic novel" notion is one minefield after another. People argue about the term itself—"the $20 word for comics," Wolk said—and when the first graphic novel appeared.

Was it 1978, with the paperback edition of Will Eisner's "A Contract With God and Other Tenement Stories: A Graphic Novel"?

Or 1895, when R.F. Outcalt's "The Yellow Kid" began his run of loosely connected adventures in *The New York World*?

Or sometime in the 11th or 12th centuries, when the Bayeux Tapestry used pictures and words to tell the tale of William the Conqueror?

Or, wonders Scott McCloud, the author of "Understanding Comics: The Invisible Art," were the ancient Egyptians the medium's pioneers? Inside the tomb of Menna, c. 1300 B.C., pictures and hieroglyphs tell a tale of farming, harvesting and tax-collecting. (As ripping yarns go, Menna's tale was no "Dark Knight.")

Then there's the question of whether "graphic novels" are literature. Support for this position has come from an unexpected and unequivocably mainstream source: *The New York Times*.

"It used to be a joke, that *The New York Times* might cover something some day," said Spurgeon of The Comics Reporter. "Now, it seems like every other week . . . ."

Remember those two Eisner nominees, mentioned earlier? *The Times* praised "American Born Chinese" in its Sunday Book Review. "Fun Home" also was reviewed there and, eight days later, in the daily newspaper. *The New York Times Magazine* serializes graphic novels—"Watergate Sue" by Megan Kelso is the current offering.

Entertainment Weekly regularly reports on graphic novels, as did *Time* until critic Arnold's resignation this March. *The New Yorker* occasionally takes note of the medium, too, but has proven a tough sell. Here's Peter Schjeldahl, writing about the late Will Eisner, the iconic figure for whom the industry named its annual awards:

Eisner created a masked-crime-fighter comic book, 'The Spirit,' in his youth; he was not a modest man, but legions of admirers forgave him that, as they forgive his work's cornball histrionics. Rooted in German Expressionism but more reminiscent of MAD-type burlesque than of George Grosz, his characters rub their hands, tear their hair, and, if they happen to fancy something, slaver.

But attention, even critical pans, are cherished by a crew that is accustomed to indifference. "There's been a real avalanche to mainstream coverage in the last, oh, five years now," Spurgeon said, "and all the bells and whistles that come with it."

One B and W: a serious re-evaluation of the art form. At Comic-Con, one panel—Sunday, 11:30 a.m. to 1 p.m.—has been dubbed "Comics Are Not Literature."

"They are not literature in the same sense that they are not painting, in the same sense that they are not cooking," said Wolk, who will moderate the panel. "Really, the crucial thing about comics is that they are *drawn*, the world filtered through an artist's eye and hand."

In fact, few "graphic novels" feature distinguished writing. There are exceptions—Joe Sacco's nonfiction work, such as "Palestine" and "The Fixer," contain tough, sometimes lyrical, prose. But in graphic novels, words are enhanced, even completed, by visuals.

At its heart, this is not a literary form. "I don't see how prose competes with comics," Spurgeon said. "That's like video competing with music."

But it is a storytelling form. Which brings us back to "Jimmy Corrigan," Chris Ware's 384-page opus, the 2001 *Guardian* Book Award winner and hailed by *The New York Times Book Review* as "arguably the greatest achievement of the form, ever."

Visually inventive, "Jimmy Corrigan" tells the story of a hapless Chicagoan, his crude—and usually absent—father and his abusive grandfather. This is not a "comic."

Wolk, the graphic novel enthusiast, calls Ware "a brilliant artist." Wolk, the would-be rumbler, notes that "Jimmy Corrigan" is studded with stylistic references to "Peanuts" and "Krazy Kat" and other classic strips. "Whatever else they did," Wolk said of these earlier works, "every single strip was meant to give pleasure. (Ware) dangles the idea of pleasure out, snatches it away and slaps you for wanting it."

But is the artist required to give pleasure?

WANTED: SHAGGINESS

Graphic novels exist in a broad range of genres: humor, romance, suspense, political satire, soap operas, horror, porn, Japanese *manga*, nonfiction journalism. In 2006, *Publishers Weekly* reported, 2,800 new titles were published. For the first time, graphic novels surpassed standard comic books in sales, $330 million to $310 million.

"The days when publishers aimed at only 15-year-old boys—or 50-year-old men who are shopping for their inner 15-year-old—those days are over," said Calvin Reid of *Publishers Weekly*.

Reid cited five reasons for the growth:

1. The Japanese invasion. *Manga*, which has delved into adult topics for decades, is the fastest-growing segment of the market. Of last year's new titles, more than 40 percent were manga.

2. Chain book stores. Barnes & Noble, Borders and others now stock graphic novels.

3. Librarians. "A new generation of librarians grew up with the underground comics of the '60s and '70s. To them, a graphic novel is just another book."

4. Hollywood. Multiplexes are stuffed with movies based on comics or cartoons—"Fantastic Four," "Spider-Man 3," "The Simpsons." Tentatively scheduled for next year: "Watchmen."

5. The Internet's retailing reach. "Comics are now available to people who don't have comic shops near them."

Surely, though, there must be some Americans who insist that comic books—even gussied up as "graphic novels"—are hopelessly lowbrow?

"I don't think there are any serious holdouts in mainstream culture," Reid said.

Tom Spurgeon hopes this isn't true. He takes comfort in the fact that comics often ignore trends that have swept the society at large. "There's not any 'Grey's Anatomy' equivalent in comics," he said. "Not an 'American Idol.'"

For Spurgeon, graphic novels require words, images and attitude. "If there is a little bit of shagginess to it," he said, "it retains its edge as an art form."

GRAPHIC NOVEL STARTER KIT

IO TO READ

Let's say you're new to graphic novels.

Let's say you're sucked into a conversation on this very subject.

Finally, let's say you're a daredevil. (But not *The* Daredevil.)

Relax. To bluff your way through this ordeal, just cite these seminal works:

1 "The Spirit," (1940s), Will Eisner.

In the 1940s, Eisner (1917–2005) combined clean lines, bold colors and realistic characters to escape the comic book industry's superhero ghetto. His "A Contract With God" (1978) is often cited as one of the first books sold as a "graphic novel." But we prefer this earlier series about a hero sans superpowers. "The Spirit" has its problems—Eisner's treatment of Ebony, an African-American boy whose intelligence is not quite obscured by his thick Southern patois, borders on the condescending. At its best, though, "Spirit" is two-fisted and sophisticated.

2) "Batman: The Dark Knight Returns," (1986), Frank Miller.

In 1986, Frank Miller radically reimagined one of comic book world's central myths. "Dark Knight" gives us an aging, angry, alienated Bruce Wayne, a figure of tarnished nobility caught in an apocalyptic struggle with villains and heroes.

3) "Watchmen," (1986–87), Alan Moore and Dave Gibbons.

Edward Blake, a retired costumed crimefighter, is murdered—and the ensuing investigation delves deep into the secrets of a band of superheroes. Gibbons' artwork is seductive and strangely familiar, but the real star is Moore's intelligent, suspenseful, rapid-fire storytelling, set in an alternative America engaged in Cold War brinksmanship. Stumbling upon "Watchmen" is like walking into your first Hitchcock; you emerge spellbound and grateful.

4) "Maus, A Survivor's Tale: My Father Bleeds History," (1986), and "Maus II, A Survivor's Tale: And Here My Troubles Began," (1991), Art Spiegelman.

Even before receiving a special Pulitzer Prize in 1992, "Maus" had expanded the discussion on comics and art. Only a great artist could take a family tale about the Holocaust, and—persuasively, brilliantly—recast it with mice, cats and pigs.

5) "Buddha," (1974–1984), Osamu Tezuka.

A manga pioneer and devotee of Walt Disney, Tezuka (1928–1989) may be best known as the author of "Astro Boy." But his skill at juggling moods—silly, profound, erotic, violent—is given a sensational workout in this epic. Originally published in Japan, "Buddha" was republished here in eight volumes, an 1,884-page biography that blends history, philosophy and only a few purely fictitious episodes.

6) "Daniel Boring," (2000), Daniel Clowes.

Bizarre and sly, this three-part tale follows the title character's search for his father and true romance. Oh, there's also his attempt to wait out the end of the world. Clowes is perhaps better known for "Ghost World," but "Boring" is the more daring work. The narrative, dreamy and deadpan, gives equal weight to every plot development, from disappointing sexual encounters to World War III.

7) "Jimmy Corrigan, or the Smartest Kid on Earth," (2000), Chris Ware.

Relentlessly downbeat account of Jimmy Corrigan, who is—as numerous critics have noted—neither a kid nor very smart. He is a put-upon sad sack whose hunt for his father ends in a curdled victory, Jimmy reunited with a bitter, petty old man. But Ware is a breathtaking artist and designer. This book has to be seen. Read? Not so much.

8) "Persepolis: The Story of a Childhood," (2003), Marjane Satrapi.

A warm yet sad account of growing up in revolutionary Iran. Satrapi, now a resident of Paris, produced this book as a member of L'Association, a now-defunct band of French guerrilla cartoonists. In her sure hands, the personal becomes political—and bittersweetly universal.

9) "Fun Home: A Family Tragicomic," (2006), Alison Bechdel.

Hear that deafening roar? That's the buzz surrounding this hand-drawn memoir, nominated for a 2007 Eisner award. Bechdel, author of the continuing series "Dykes to Watch Out For," grew up with a discontented mother and a closeted gay father who ran a funeral home. Thanks to Bechdel's humor and love for her family, "Fun Home" takes a grim tale and turns it into something strangely hopeful.

10) "American Born Chinese," (2006), Gene Luen Yang.

Like "Fun Home," "ABC" is a coming-of-age tale that arrives at Comic-Con with a 2007 Eisner nomination. The artwork? Evocative. The dialogue? Priceless.

Teacher: "Class, I'd like us all to give a warm Mayflower Elementary welcome to your new friend and classmate Jing Jang!"

Jin Wang: "Jin Wang."

Teacher: "Jin Wang! He and his family recently moved to our neighborhood all the way from China!"

Jin Wang: "San Francisco."

3

Comics in the Classroom:
Using Graphic Novels to Improve Literacy

Editor's Introduction

As comics and graphic novels have gained acceptance among mainstream readers, they have also made an impression on educators. Many librarians and teachers are now incorporating them into their lessons, often as a means of engaging reluctant readers, at other times to challenge more gifted students. Most of the articles in this chapter come from educational journals—a testament to comics' usefulness in promoting literacy.

In "Comics in the Classroom," this chapter's first selection, Laura Hudson examines how such comic-book publishers as DC Comics and Dark Horse have set their sights on the school market. Hudson also explains why educators need specific teaching guides and other tools to help them select age-appropriate graphic novels and properly integrate them into their curricula.

The next piece, "Going Graphic," finds educator and graphic-novel specialist James Bucky Carter debunking common misconceptions about graphic novels. Carter argues that comics don't constitute a single genre, and that they can be used to tell many different types of stories. He also insists that comics are neither "kid stuff" nor useful only for teaching reluctant readers. He says students of all ages and reading levels can benefit from not only reading graphic novels, but also creating their own.

In the following article, "Using Comics and Graphic Novels in the Classroom," scholars and teachers discuss how graphic novels can help teach basic grammar, encourage creative writing, and expose students to different types of literature.

In "'The Best of Both Worlds': Rethinking the Literary Merit of Graphic Novels," Sean P. Connors, an assistant professor of English education at the University of Arkansas, Fayetteville, argues that graphic novels should be read as literature and not merely used to promote literacy. Connors calls on scholarly journals to better scrutinize graphic novels and help educators select titles worthy of the classroom.

Gretchen Schwarz, in the subsequent piece, "Expanding Literacies through Graphic Novels," places graphic novels in the context of the nontraditional forms of literacy experts believe today's students need to master. "Both traditional, alphabetic literacy and literacies such as information, visual, and media literacy can be well served by classroom engagement with the graphic novel," Schwarz writes. "The graphic novel is a medium that combines the visual and verbal as do films,

TV, and even pop-up ads. The graphic novel, however, holds still and allows special attention to be given to its unique visual and word arrangement."

Comics in the Classroom[*][1]

Thanks to a New Generation of Educators, the School and Library Markets Keep on Growing

By Laura Hudson
Publishers Weekly, December 22, 2008

There was once a time not so long ago when the only way comics made their way into classrooms was surreptitiously—hidden in backpacks or behind the textbooks of daydreaming students. But in many schools and universities around the nation, the attitudes of educators toward comics have been turned upside down.

Long ghettoized—even demonized—in North America as puerile and pulpy, both "comic books" (traditional comics periodicals) and book-format graphic novels are now being used in both k–12 and higher education classrooms as everything from early developmental reading tools to serious literary texts.

Partly, the shift is a recognition that the medium of comics has grown up, with graphic novels now claiming significant space on library shelves. Titles like *Maus*, *Fun Home* and *American Born Chinese* have won literary awards normally reserved for prose novels, and an increasing number of educators-cum-comics fans now work within their institutions as thoughtful advocates for the medium.

According to Milton Griepp, CEO of the pop culture news site ICv2.com, and Diamond Comics sales manager John Shableski, sales of graphic novels to libraries and schools increased from about $1 million in 2001 to more than $30 million in 2007, spurring many comics publishers to eye the unfamiliar multibillion-dollar educational publishing industry with increasing interest.

1 Author's note: For more information on the issues covered in this article, see my presentation for the New Hampshire Council of Teachers of English at www.archive.org/details/NhcteTalk08GraphicNovels.

LIBRARIAN ADVOCACY KEY

Educator and comics specialist Peter Gutierrez attributes much of the growing interest from schools to the support and advocacy of librarians, many of whom responded to growing mainstream interest in graphic novels by developing significant library collections. "In the last two years, there's been an explosion of interest, spurred by the popularity and obvious quality of graphic novels in libraries. It's created more fertile ground for the kind of lateral movement of sequential art narratives into the classroom itself," says Gutierrez.

"The schools market is a sleeping giant, and it's about to wake up," Shableski says. "NCTE [National Council of Teachers of English] is the big conference, attended by 8,000 to 9,000 English teachers. Historically, they've had one or two programs out of 300 where they mention graphic novels or comics. Last year there were eight. This year at San Antonio, there [were] 11 dedicated graphic novel programs. That's a big thing in the educational market."

Most major comics companies are now dipping a toe into the schools market, and while some have made only cursory attempts to reach teachers, others, such as Dark Horse Comics, have worked directly with academics and education experts to develop materials. The publishing home of Hellboy and Sin City, Dark Horse also publishes materials for an educational comics initiative called the Comic Book Project, developed by Columbia University Teaching School professor Michael Bitz in 2001 to reinforce literacy by teaching kids to develop, script and draw their own comics.

"There are currently about 900 [Comic Book Project] programs across the country," says Dark Horse marketing coordinator Aaron Colter, who adds that participation in the program has been increasing. "We've had about 115 schools adopt it this year alone, and 30 in the last three months."

But for every publisher working side by side with educators or attending American Library Association conferences, others have made only perfunctory attempts to reach out. "It's great that there's some material for teaching graphic novels, but they aren't really comparable to what a typical language arts teacher would expect from an educational publisher or trade publisher," Gutierrez says. "In graphic novels, publishers don't have the expertise or the money to invest in research or teaching guides. They're waiting to see if the market justifies that kind of incursion, while the educators are waiting for more third-party-verified research studies."

NEW MARKET A CHALLENGE

The biggest question mark is not just whether educators will accept comics as teaching materials on a broader scale, but whether traditional comics publishers, who only began to get their graphic novels into the general bookstore market in the last 10 years, are prepared to capitalize on the opportunity.

"Comics publishers are lagging behind traditional book publishers," says Janna Morishima, director of the Diamond Kids Group at Diamond Comics Distributors. "Creating for kids hasn't been a big priority until rather recently. I think they're still getting used to the book market, and the educational market is an even more specialized part of the market. They are at a bit of a disadvantage."

For DC Comics, home of Superman and Batman and, with Marvel, one of the "Big Two" mainstream comics publishers, the most efficient way to deal with their relative lack of expertise in educational publishing was simply to switch to a distributor that already possessed it. DC moved from Hachette to Random House Distribution in 2007.

"This discussion of how to expand our market was a crucial factor when we moved distribution. One of the more impressive things in the Random House package was the systems they have to access the school and library markets," says John Cunningham, v-p of marketing at DC Comics. "Understanding their needs and how to sell and market to them is an enormously complex undertaking. Plugging our materials into [Random House's] system made more sense than trying to develop systems of our own."

For publishers who don't have the option of signing on with a distribution giant like Random House, however, industry experts say there are still plenty of ways to make inroads into classrooms, often by starting simply.

"Connect with the teachers who are using your titles, and they will be your low-cost or no-cost guides to this terra incognita," Gutierrez says. "You probably have an enthusiastic pathfinder and guide in the educators out there, who would love to tell you how they're using your material. If you don't have that conversation to gather feedback from k–12 educators, you're really doing message-in-a-bottle advertising and just throwing stuff out there."

EVALUATING VISUAL LITERACY

Many teachers who want to use comics in k–12 classrooms say that they need more information about graphic novels in order to evaluate them as teaching materials, ranging from age recommendations and teaching guides to more complex measures, like Lexile scores—tools that most comics publishers don't provide.

At least one comics publisher has taken that advice to heart and has created comprehensively researched and educator-tested comics works for use in the classroom. Toon Books, an imprint founded by Françoise Mouly, art editor of the New Yorker, publishes titles for children in kindergarten through third grade that were developed and tested with the hands-on help of teachers and reading specialists.

"The intent of Toon Books was specifically to provide comics for children who are just learning to read. That's a very specific step in the development of the kids. You have to acknowledge that if you are publishing for children, you have to select an age level and vocabulary that has been vetted for degree of difficulty," Mouly says. "This is a very different set of knowledge. I worked very hard with educators editorially, going to various schools and watching the kids reading our books, so that we didn't take anything for granted."

Toon Books was also among the first graphic novel publishers to analyze its books using the Lexile scale, a system designed to measure the difficulty of a text and help teachers assess its suitability for students at different reading levels. Although an external measure of academic rigor could potentially add credibility to comics in the eyes of teachers, the Lexile system is designed to assess only text, ignoring the visual component in a medium where images and words are inextricably linked. "It's evaluating [the text] as though there are no visual cues. It's apples and oranges in terms of what that means," says Peter Coogan, director of the Institute for Comics Studies.

The visual component of comics may be difficult to quantify, but it is also part of what makes comics a valuable learning tool, particularly in an increasingly image-oriented world. "We're a visual culture now, not a typographical culture," Coogan says. "Comics teach visual literacy."

Literacy isn't simply being able to understand the written word, Mouly explains, but "being able to extract meaning from a printed page. There's a kind of visual literacy that is innate. There's a lot that kids are able to understand and an enormous amount of complexity that can be used. It's like poetry: deceptively simple, and levels and levels of meaning can be brought out."

At the same time, English and Language Arts teachers often have no training in visual narratives and need to learn new skill sets. Even those teachers who are enthusiastic about using comics face other institutional obstacles, such as the testing demands of the federal No Child Left Behind law, as well as any state or institutional requirements.

"I think that many teachers want to value comics and graphic novels in their classrooms, but are not sure how to do so," notes Katie Monnin, an assistant professor at the University of North Florida who is researching ways for teachers to integrate visual literacy into standards-based classes. "Since there are so many federal mandates on their curricula, they want to make sure that they are teaching all of their goals and standards."

Although comics programs in public schools may leave some superintendents dubious for that very reason, they need only look at the Comic Book Initiative in the state of Maryland for a model of a comics program that can work in standards-based classrooms. Five years ago, the Maryland State Department of Education launched a pilot program in a few school districts to teach lesson plans based on comics from a toolkit developed by Disney. The lessons were integrated into the voluntary portion of the state curriculum, and developed with extensive input from principals and teachers. "It was very vetted," says Darla Strouse, director of the Comic Book Initiative.

An in-depth evaluation by the University of Maryland examined the motivational impact of using comics in the classroom, through focus groups of teachers, students, and parents. Strouse says, "It came back very positive. [The students] won't put their hands down. You start with graphic novels and they're so excited."

By the summer of 2008, the program's success led to its expansion from eight schools to 160 schools, with similarly positive results. Although Strouse says that adopting a comics program might have been difficult without a supportive superintendent, she believes that Maryland "can be a jump start for other states" to launch similar projects.

Outside of the k–12 level, graphic novels and comics have also made their way into university classrooms, where they have been adopted as course texts in a variety of disciplines. "There's a critical mass of [professors] who are pursuing this as a study, and they're legitimizing the medium not only for their students but also for their departments," says Coogan, adding, however, that many comics publishers doom their chances for course adoptions by their unwillingness to send free copies to professors.

"Comics publishers could be actively trying to cultivate relationships with university English departments," suggests Aaron Kashtan, a teaching assistant who researches comics theory at the University of Florida. "At my university, the English department regularly holds book fairs where textbook publishers like Penguin and McGraw-Hill market their materials to the department's instructors. These publishers do this because for each instructor who decides to adopt a textbook, 20-some students will then have to buy that textbook. Comics publishers don't seem to have come to a similar realization that university students represent an untapped source of income."

Top Shelf Productions co-publisher Chris Staros explains it this way, "If 100 university courses with 40 students each use a book on a regular basis, that's 4,000 copies a year." In the comics industry, where sales of the top graphic novels often run under 10,000 copies, those sales can constitute a significant base.

Coogan suggests that comics publishers still willing to ignore the sales potential of the educational market in favor of their established fan base might find it in their interest to take a longer view. "Comics are graying in many ways; there aren't many eight-year-olds reading comics. Kids have so much media to experience now, there's no guarantee kids will be exposed to comics. If comics aren't careful as an industry, they're going to become a nostalgia item for a niche market. Teaching comics definitely brings in new readers."

HUDSON *is a senior editor at the* Comic Foundry *magazine and a contributor to* PW Comics Week.

Going Graphic*

Understanding What Graphic Novels Are—and Aren't—Can Help Teachers Make the Best Use of This Literary Form

By James Bucky Carter
Educational Leadership, March 2009

As a graphic novel specialist and teacher educator, I travel across the United States sharing information on how teachers can use this media in their classrooms to expand student literacy skills. The questions, comments, and occasional resistance I've encountered have led me to conclude that some misinformation concerning the pedagogical potential of graphic novels is circulating among teachers. Some believe that graphic novels are too risky to bring into the curriculum, others resist any form of new literacy altogether, and many think that sequential art narratives are only useful for remedial or reluctant readers. To clear up these misconceptions, I'd like to share a few facts about the form and a few practical suggestions for teachers considering integrating graphic novels into their classes.

AS OLD AS CAVE PAINTINGS

Sequential art narratives—broadly defined as images placed in sequence to tell a story—have been steadily gaining attention over the last couple of decades as teachers, literacy experts, and librarians have sought new means to engage reluctant readers and inspire more motivated ones. Practitioners and researchers have found these texts, usually published as graphic novels or comic books, to be of great use in increasing library circulation, creating new readers, helping English language learners, motivating male readers, and even assisting gifted and talented students. In many ways, it seems that the graphic novel as accepted pedagogical text has "arrived."

Actually, comics are not a new phenomenon, nor are the attempts to connect them to education. Some would argue that sequential art narratives date back to the earliest cave paintings. Comic books, which grew out of the newspaper comic strips that gained popularity in the 1880s and 1890s, have existed in the United States since the 1920s. Superhero comics debuted in 1938 with *Action Comics #1*, the first appearance of Superman. Not even the recently popular Japanese import comics, Manga, are 21st-century inventions.

There is a long history of the form being used for teaching, including hieroglyphics, tapestries, and stained glass windows (McCloud, 1999). M. Thomas Inge's *Comics as Culture* (1990), Bradford Wright's *Comic Book Nation* (2001), and Steven Krashen's *The Power of Reading* (2004) all cite studies from education and sociological journals that date back at least to the late 1930s. The term graphic novel has been in use in the United States since around 1964 and gained widespread recognition in 1978 when Will Eisner prominently placed the term on the cover of the paperback edition of *A Contract with God and Other Tenement Stories*. Although teachers have paid more attention to sequential art narration of late, comics and graphic novels are better considered as "new to you" rather than literally new.

AN ART FORM, NOT A GENRE

Another misconception is that graphic novels and comics are a genre of literature (Carter, 2008). Westerns, romances, science fiction, and fantasy are genres. *All-American Western*, *All True Romance*, *Star Trek*, and *Sandman* are comics that feature each of these genres, respectively. This distinction is important because teachers may be more willing to use sequential art narratives to supplement existing curriculums by looking for genre connections rather than teaching comics in isolation. In fact, I believe that integrating comics into existing thematic units can be more effective than studying the form in isolation.

Studying how a graphic novelist frames a story benefits students' developing sense of craft and composition. Comparing how Art Spiegelman uses words and art to tell about his family's experiences during the Holocaust in *Maus* to the conventions that Elie Wiesel or Lois Lowry or Anne Frank (or all of them) use when writing about the same topic is even better. Teachers should weigh their decision to teach comics through study units focusing solely on the form with the possibly more expansive and connection-building method of using this material to supplement existing curriculums.

NOT JUST FOR RELUCTANT READERS

Much recent attention to graphic novels results from the admirable efforts of librarians who noticed drastic increases in circulation once graphic novels were added to their libraries. Articles from their professional literature often proclaim that young people who never saw themselves as readers suddenly devoured books once they were exposed to graphic novels. On the basis of these claims, educators began using graphic novels to engage low-level or reluctant readers.

There is evidence that certain populations (boys, for example) prefer visual texts over those without visual elements (Smith & Wilhelm, 2002) and that allowing students to read comics may engage students who are otherwise less interested or less proficient in English (Cary, 2004). Research has also shown that comic book readers have a tendency to read more varied texts and that comic book reading often acts as a gateway to both more reading and more varied reading (Krashen, 2004).

Comics do have potential to motivate reluctant readers, but the study of sequential art can also benefit students who are already motivated readers. For example, Mitchell and George (1996) used superhero comics to examine morality and ethical issues with gifted students, and I have observed teachers using graphic novels as literature with honors-level seniors. I have used sequential art texts with students of various reading levels with an age range that extends from 6th grade to graduate school.

NOT NECESSARILY "KID STUFF"

Another assumption that may prevent teachers from sharing worthwhile comics with older and more motivated students or that may lead teachers to make unwise decisions about appropriateness in the classroom is that comics are written for a young audience. The notion that comic books are for children is long-standing, and surely young people have always been drawn to them.

But, countering these assumptions, exemplary graphic novels of the past 30 years have dealt with such mature topics as date rape, teen pregnancy, the Iraq war, Hurricane Katrina, genocide, and gang violence, as well as all of the major issues that adolescents face: coming of age, identity formation, friendship, and change. Even superhero comics have explored such weighty issues as drug addiction, mental illness, HIV infection, and land mine safety.

Teachers can make mistakes easily when they assume that all comic book-style productions are for children. At a recent talk in Normal, Illinois, a teacher told me that a local 4th grade teacher was having her students read *Persepolis*, a wonderful coming-of-age story about a young woman dealing with the Iranian revolution of the 1970s and 1980s. Although there are parts of the novel where the narrator is at the equivalent age of a U.S. 4th grader, there are also explicit visual depictions of violence. I'm a proponent of the form and an advocate of this particular text, but even I think this graphic novel may be too much, too fast for elementary students. Teachers who assume that cartoony images or simplified drawings like those in *Persepolis* signify age- or grade-level appropriateness tread on dangerous ground.

I strongly urge teachers to use appropriate procedures for integrating graphic texts into the classroom, just as they would for more traditional texts. Writing rationales for texts that someone is likely to challenge is a smart way for teachers to help protect their students, themselves, their parents, and their school leaders, and this is especially true for graphic novels. After all, they are graphic in that they have a pictorial element. Consider what Steven Cary (2004) calls the *naked buns effect*, a term he uses to describe the likely difference in reaction to the words "naked buns" in a letter-based text versus the reaction to an image of naked buns.

To effectively and responsibly use graphic novels in their classes, teachers must not simply trust the often excellent reviews in the *ALAN Review* or *Voices of Youth Advocate*. They must read every page and every panel of a graphic novel or comic, weigh it against their understanding of community standards, then decide whether to bring the material into the classroom.

Consider the recent case of Connecticut English teacher Nate Fisher, who asked a 14-year-old female student to read a copy of comics pioneer Daniel Clowes's *Eightball*, which includes a sequence featuring a blue rabbit walking the streets of his town asking for sexual favors. Fisher may have forgotten about this section, or he may have misread his community's standards, but the resultant complaints from the girl's parents ended up with him being fired. Things might have been different if Fisher had paperclipped to the text a rationale or note seeking a parent signature.

I do not share this story to discourage teachers from using graphic novels in their classes. I simply urge teachers to act responsibly. Writing rationales that support the book, that discuss any controversial material and how it is handled in the text and will be addressed in class, and that offer parents and students a chance to preview and discuss the reading choice before signing off on it can provide a measure of comfort and protection to all.

This gets to another issue of use: Teachers needn't use a graphic novel in full to feel the medium's power. For example, another of Clowes's excellent graphic novels, *Ghost World*, details the life of two recent high school graduates and best friends who are now pondering their futures. Although there are sexually explicit scenes that may disqualify the text from whole-class reading, there are also several sequences of panels in which the two friends discuss growing apart that are appropriate for sharing with almost every student. Although a teacher may not care to share the entirety of Gareth Hinds's excellent graphic novel of *Beowulf*, sharing a few pages of the artist's visualization of Grendel or the dragon can help bring the characters and the story alive. Even one powerful panel can help establish or reinforce a major theme and be a jumping-off point for discussion and further literacy-related activities.

CREATING COMICS

Another concept that often goes unconsidered is that comics and graphic novels needn't only be integrated into the curriculum as additional reading material. Accepting them as books is a nice start, but writing and drawing graphic novels is an authentic composing activity. By acknowledging that there is a process behind the production of comics and asking students to consider the process and even engage in it, teachers help students build crafting, composing, viewing, and visualizing skills.

I have noted teachers using Comic Life software to create their own photocomic stories. Michael Bitz (2004), founder of the Comic Book Project, teamed with Dark Horse Comics to get paper-based comic page templates into the hands of students across the eastern United States. Bitz found that when students learn the composing techniques associated with the comics form, they tell compelling stories that often connect to students' lived experiences and actual social worlds, rather than to capes and tights.

Recently, teacher Diana Weidenbacker and students from Winnacunnet High School in New Hampshire presented me with an anthology of sequential art short stories entitled *Scars*. Each story revolves around the theme of impression: "Scars, we all have them. Some are small cuts that we got falling off our bikes, others. . . . Others are deeper and recede from the surface only to reappear at moments when we least expect them." Weidenbacker and her 15 students used simple templates from Comic Book Creator and Microsoft Word, as well as pencils, markers, crayons, and basic photocopying and binding techniques to produce an authentic and heartfelt exploration of the hard times in their lives.

I have used a lesson approved by the National Council of Teachers of English and the International Reading Association titled the Comic Book Show and Tell (Carter, 2006, 2007) to teach students the conventions of comic book scripting. Students create a script based on a generic prompt and pass their scripts to partners across the room who must draw panels guided by nothing more than the authors' written words. When students receive their scripts back with the artists' interpretation, the students have a visual record of how detailed and descriptive their script was, and I help them to revise their products accordingly. I have used this activity with 6th graders, high schoolers, and even preservice teachers. Educators have also asked students to produce "how-to" comics and graphic novel biographies of famous people, works that can be collected and shared with other students.

A WELL-ROUNDED LITERACY

The National Council of Teachers of English and the International Reading Association (1996) define the English language arts as reading, writing, speaking, listening, visualizing, and visually representing. Their standards require that students be capable of recognizing and studying a variety of genres and forms and suggest a broad definition of text, reading, and literacy.

Reading specialists and scholars speak again and again to the need for authentic reading and writing experiences, textual investigations that help bridge the gap between the school world and the lived world, between narrow notions of what it means to be literate and broad notions of what it means to actually succeed as an intelligent adult in contemporary society. The effective use of graphic novels and other forms of sequential art can help teachers accomplish all of these goals. When paired with other forms, old and new, this ancient type of text can be a valuable bridge between student and text, student and teacher, and the centuries themselves.

NOTABLE GRAPHIC NOVELS

These are just a few of the excellent graphic novels that teachers might consider sharing with students.

FOR ELEMENTARY STUDENTS

Big Fat Little Lit, edited by Art Spiegelman and Francoise Mouly (Puffin, 2006). This anthology of the best from the *Little Lit* series features fairy tales, fables, scary stories, and bedtime reading fare by such authors and artists as Neil Gaiman, David Sedaris, Maurice Sendak, and Lemony Snicket.

Bone: The Complete Comic in One Volume, by Jeff Smith (Cartoon Books, 2004). This 1,300-pager is a classic fantasy tale featuring three cartoonish cousins, puppy love, and a quest to save a kingdom.

FOR MIDDLE SCHOOL STUDENTS

American Born Chinese, by Gene Luen Yang (First Second, 1997). This Printz-award-winning triptych weaves together a coming-of-age narrative, Eastern mythology, and a sitcom-style story of contemporary teen life.

Chiggers, by Hope Larson (Aladdin, 2008). This tale of summer camp portrays challenges and changes in one teen girl's friendships.

Goodbye, Chunky Rice, by Craig Thompson (Pantheon, 2006). Thompson's touching sea adventure acts as a backdrop for deconstructing the pasts of his cartoonish but deep characters and the emotional resonance driving them in the present.

Kid Beowulf and the Blood-Bound Oath, by Alexis E. Fajardo (Bowler Hat Comics, 2008). This primer on the epic form, slated to be a 12-book series, takes the classic tale and reworks it in ways sure to get readers invested in the characters by the time they read the poem in high school.

FOR HIGH SCHOOL STUDENTS

The Best American Comics 2008, edited by Lynda Barry (Houghton Mifflin, 2008). This excellent anthology features a host of genres and top comics creators.

The Complete Persepolis, by Marjane Satrapi (Pantheon, 2007). Now also a feature film, Marjane Satrapi's autobiography shares as much history of the Middle East as it does of her own growth from precocious child to expressive adult.

Pride of Baghdad, by Brian K. Vaughan and Niko Henrichon (DC Comics, 2006). *The Lion King* meets the U.S. Armed Forces in this based-on-true-events tale of lions roaming the Iraqi countryside after a bomb destroys their zoo.

The Tale of One Bad Rat, by Brian Talbot (Dark Horse, 1995). This tastefully crafted narrative stars a young female lead coming to terms with sexual abuse by her father.

REFERENCES

Bitz, M. (2004). The comic book project: Forging alternative pathways to literacy. *Journal of Adolescent and Adult Literacy, 47*, 574–586.

Carter, J. B. (2006). *The comic book show and tell*. Newark, DE: International Reading Association. Available: www.readwritethink.org/lessons/lesson_view.asp?id=921

Carter, J. B. (2007). Ultimate Spider-Man and student-generated classics: Using graphic novels and comics to produce authentic voice and detailed, authentic texts. In J. B. Carter (Ed.), *Building literacy connections with graphic novels: Page by page, panel by panel* (pp. 145–155). Urbana, IL: National Council of Teachers of English.

Carter, J. B. (2008). Die a graphic death: Revisiting the death of genre with graphic novels, or "Why won't you just die already?" *The ALAN Review, 36*(1), 15–25.

Cary, S. (2004). *Going graphic: Comics at work in the multilingual classroom*. Portsmouth, NH: Heinemann.

Inge, M. T. (1990). *Comics as culture*. Jackson: University Press of Mississippi.

Krashen, S. D. (2004). *The power of reading: Insights from the research* (2nd ed.). Westport, CT: Libraries Unlimited.

McCloud, S. (1999). *Understanding comics*. New York: DC Comics.

Mitchell, J. P., & George, J. D. (1996). What do Superman, Captain America, and Spider-man have in common? The case for comic books. *Gifted Education International, 11,* 91–94.

National Council of Teachers of English & International Reading Association. (1996). *Standards for the English language arts.* Urbana, IL: National Council of Teachers of English.

Smith, M. W., & Wilhelm, J. D. (2002). *Reading don't fix no Chevys.* Portsmouth, NH: Heinemann.

Wright, B. (2001). *Comic book nation.* Baltimore, MD: Johns Hopkins Press.

Author's note: For more information on the issues covered in this article, see my presentation for the New Hampshire Council of Teachers of English at www.archive.org/details/NhcteTalk08GraphicNovels.

JAMES BUCKY CARTER *is Assistant Professor of English Education at the University of Texas at El Paso; jbcarter2@utep.edu. He is the editor of* Building Literacy Connections with Graphic Novels: Page by Page, Panel by Panel *(National Council of Teachers of English, 2007).*

Using Comics and Graphic Novels in the Classroom[*]

The Council Chronicle, September 2005

While Americans tend to view comics as "fodder for children," people in Europe and Japan have a more positive view of the medium, explains John Lowe, who is chair of the Sequential Art Department at the Savannah College of Art and Design in Georgia. Lowe thinks comics deserve more credit, especially since they launched his interest in literature.

"I started reading comics, and then I got into other types of fiction and literature. I stopped reading comics a little later, but I don't think I would have made the leap [to literature] if it weren't for comics." In his case, Lowe says, he literally went from reading "Batman to Faulkner."

Now he works with students who are interested in cartoons, graphic novels, and manga—Japanese comics and graphic novels—which Lowe notes are especially popular among female students. He has seen a steady increase of interest in the school's sequential art offering since the program started to take shape in the early nineties.

Storytelling is the program's primary focus because this skill prepares students to work in any genre, Lowe explains. He adds that the demands are tough and require "a high level of concentration and skill—such as writing, drawing, inking, and having computer coloring skills."

BRIDGING LITERACIES

Other educators also see the educational potential of comics and graphic novels. They can help with building complex reading skills, according to Shelley Hong Xu, associate professor in the department of teacher education at California State University, Long Beach. She says that graphic novels and comics should have a classroom role similar to children's literature.

Comics and graphic novels can be used as a "point of reference" to bridge what students already know with what they have yet to learn, Xu says. For example, comics and graphic novels can teach about making inferences, since readers must rely on pictures and just a small amount of text. By helping students transfer this skill, she says, teachers can lessen the challenge of a new book.

Xu uses comics and graphic novels in her reading methods course. She asks preservice teachers to read an unfamiliar comic or graphic novel and then record the strategies they used to comprehend the text. "I think that every preservice and inservice teacher needs to experience this activity in order to better understand literacy knowledge and skills that students use with reading comics and graphic novels."

Xu cautions teachers to do some research before rushing to include comics and graphic novels in their teaching plans. This includes finding out about students' experiences with comics and graphic novels and studying the genre in general. She also urges teachers to respect students' enjoyment of comics and graphic novels and to view them not as "instructional materials" but as "tools for bridging" in- and out-of-school literacy experiences.

Xu further recommends that teachers talk with school administrators and parents about how using comics and graphic novels—or any texts from popular culture—can "address curriculum standards, motivate students to learn, enhance students' learning, and provide additional opportunities for those who struggle with literacy tasks."

FOCUS ON GRAPHIC NOVELS

Cat Turner, a secondary English specialist and teacher at Henry Wise Wood High School in Calgary, Alberta, recommends that teachers who want to know more about graphic novels read *Understanding Comics: The Invisible Art* by Scott McCloud and Will Eisner's *Comics and Sequential Art*.

Turner has worked with Liz Spittal, a differentiated learning and teaching specialist for the Calgary Board of Education, to determine "what makes [graphic novels] different from comics, picture books, and novels with supplementary visuals."

They found that like novels, graphic novels have a beginning, middle, and end as well as a main character that develops through conflicts and the story's climax. "The most significant difference from a comic is that the graphic novel's text is both written and visual," Turner explains. "Every part of each frame plays a role in the interpretation of the text, and hence, graphic novels actually demand sophisticated readers."

Turner adds, "Manga are very popular with our students, so much so that many students are actually learning Japanese so that they can read the newest manga straight off the press, instead of waiting for translations."

Turner and Spittal asked students to create guidebooks to help teachers understand graphic novels. They piloted the assignment in a twelfth-grade classroom and with eleventh-grade International Baccalaureate students, feeling it would "be a disservice to the genre to designate it for only the low-achieving students."

Turner and Spittal selected a range of fiction and nonfiction graphic novels and didn't include any superhero texts because they "wanted the students to treat the genre seriously." They reviewed the texts for appropriateness and weeded out some that they felt "were a little too risqué." Then they let students follow their own interests in choosing a novel.

The results were fantastic, says Turner, who is a member of the English Language Arts Council of the Alberta Teachers' Association. "Not only did the students become the experts, but they also demonstrated their awareness of the craftsmanship that goes into each of these texts through the creation of the guides."

Turner and Spittal noted the genre's growing popularity when they went to check out graphic novels from the Calgary library and found there were over 350 titles in a collection that continues to grow.

COMICS ART GROUP EXPANDING RESOURCES

Interest in comics and graphic novels as well as questions about how to use them in the classroom have encouraged the National Association of Comics Art Educators (http://www.teachingcomics.org) to gear up for a new initiative to help K–12 teachers and librarians understand and use the texts.

Ben Towle helped to found the group that started a few years ago "to further the cause of teaching the art form" in colleges and "to serve as a depot for exchanging ideas, lessons, tips, and experiences."

Towle believes that the concept of using comics and graphic novels in the classroom is at the stage that the discipline of film studies was in the 1950s and 60s: "It was becoming a movement." He feels the medium itself is going through a renaissance, with academic interest being one reflection of this.

TEACHING PUNCTUATION, PARAGRAPHING, AND OUTLINING

Using comics and graphic novels in the classroom is about harnessing students' natural interests, explains Rachael Sawyer Perkins, a teacher at Dolores Street Elementary School in Carson, California. She also believes that it's a way to teach important reading and writing skills.

"For students who lack the ability to visualize as they read, it provides a graphic sense that approximates what good readers do as they read. Moreover, it provides an excellent way for reluctant writers to communicate a story that has a beginning, middle, and end. I think comics and graphic novels are an excellent vehicle for teaching writing, as a story has to be pared down to its most basic elements. It is easy for the students to look at a short comic strip and identify story elements."

Perkins uses comics to teach punctuation for dialogue, and sees them as "an extremely visual way of getting across the concept of using quotation marks around narrative text spoken by individuals. The students knew that each time they saw a dialogue balloon it meant the text inside was spoken and needed to be placed in quotation marks."

Perkins also finds that cartoons are an effective way to teach outlining skills. "Using a comic, the students were able to understand that each panel represented a paragraph. The narrative text at the top became the topic sentence of sorts, communicating the main idea of the paragraph. The details were found in the visuals and in the dialogue."

LEARNING LITERARY TERMS

Sharon F. Webster, English department chairperson and literacy coach at Narragansett High School in Narragansett, Rhode Island, believes that comics can engage students in the pre-reading stage and can serve as a connection through the reading and assessment stages.

Webster says that when she uses comics and music to teach the concept of transcendentalism, students gain a better understanding of the concept. "The quality of their understanding came through in the connections they then made to the work of Emerson and Thoreau." (Find her lesson, "Examining Transcendentalism through Popular Culture," on the ReadWriteThink Web site at http://www. readwritethink.org.)

She also uses comics to teach literary terms. "Many of today's comics rely heavily on allusion, satire, irony, and parody to make a point. Students discover they might actually need to know such terms for reasons other than analyzing a Dickinson poem. Making this connection has strengthened their understanding of terms."

However, Webster believes people often miss the sophistication of comics. "Lurking beneath the literal meaning of strips like 'Shoe,' 'Calvin and Hobbes,' and even 'Zits' is the chance to capture the curiosity of a student who might never have otherwise given a term like existentialism a glance. We need to take advantage of every learning opportunity to engage our students in a way that acknowledges the visual world in which they live."

"The Best of Both Worlds"[*]

Rethinking the Literary Merit of Graphic Novels

By Sean P. Connors
The ALAN Review, Summer 2010

> The future of this form awaits its participants who truly believe that the application of sequential art, with its interweaving of words and pictures, could provide a dimension of communication that contributes—hopefully on a level never before attained—to the body of literature that concerns itself with the examination of human experience.
> —Will Eisner, *Comics and Sequential Art* (p. 141)

To say that graphic novels have attracted attention from educators is by now axiomatic. Professional journals, like this one, routinely feature articles that extol their virtue as a pedagogical tool. Books attest to the creative ways teachers are using them to scaffold students as readers and writers. Sessions devoted to graphic novels at the National Council of Teachers of English's annual convention are invariably well attended and seem to proliferate in number from one year to the next. By all accounts, it would seem that educators have embraced a form of text whose older brother, the comic book, was scorned by teachers in the not-so-distant past. Appearances, however, can be deceiving.

When Melanie Hundley, on behalf of the editors of *The ALAN Review*, invited me to contribute a column on graphic novels for an issue of the journal devoted to the influence of film, new media, digital technology, and the image on young adult literature, I was only too happy to oblige because it afforded me the opportunity to confront two assumptions that strike me as characterizing arguments for using graphic novels in schools: the first is that graphic novels are a means to an end, an assumption that usually results in overlooking their literary merit; the second assumes that students will embrace graphic novels enthusiastically, in spite of the stigmas attached to them.

Consider, for a moment, some of the reasons educators are encouraged to embrace graphic novels—and, to a lesser extent, comic books—as a teaching tool. Graphic novels are said to:
- scaffold students for whom reading and writing are difficult (Ritz, 2004; Frey & Fisher, 2004; Morrison, Bryan, & Chilcoat, 2002);
- foster visual literacy (Frey & Fisher, 2008);
- support English language learners (Ranker, 2007);
- motivate "reluctant" readers (Crawford, 2004; Dorrell, 1987);
- and provide a stepping stone that leads students to transact with more traditional (and presumably more valuable) forms of literature.

These are worthwhile objectives, and it is not hard to understand why a form of text thought to lend itself to addressing so many ends would capture the imagination of educators. At the same time, these arguments strike me as perpetuating—albeit unintentionally—a misperception that has plagued the comic book for the better part of its existence. Specifically, it regards works written in the medium of comics (be it comic books or graphic novels) as a less complex, less sophisticated form of reading material best used with weaker readers or struggling students.

It is tempting to interpret the enthusiasm literacy educators have shown for graphic novels as a sign of the field's having moved toward a broader understanding of what "counts" as text—surely our willingness to embrace a form of reading material similar to one our predecessors demonized is evidence of a more progressive, if not more enlightened, view. To be sure, there was no shortage of teachers and librarians who lined up to denounce the comic book when adolescents laid claim to it as a part of youth culture in the 1940s and 1950s. Less frequently acknowledged is that there were also educators who adopted a more tolerant view of the comic book and who sought to use students' interest in it as a foundation on which to develop their literacy practices and literary tastes. By examining the professional debate that raged over comic books in the 1940s, it is possible to appreciate the extent to which current arguments for using graphic novels in the classroom parallel those educators made on behalf of the comic book in the past.

Parents and educators paid relatively little attention to the comic book when Superman made his debut in Action Comics in 1938. Within two years, however, the commercial success the character experienced, coupled with the legion of imitators he spawned, made it difficult for them to do so any longer. David Hadju (2008) observes that the number of comic books published in the United States grew from 150 in 1937 to approximately 700 in 1940 (p. 34). While the connection adults drew between comic books and juvenile delinquency would gain traction in the early 1950s, much of the early criticism leveled against comic books focused on their perceived aesthetic value—or lack thereof. Sterling North, a literary critic for the *Chicago Daily News*, was one of the first to question the propriety of allowing adolescents to read comic books. In an editorial published on May 8, 1940, titled "A National Disgrace," he chastised the comic book for, among other things, being "badly drawn, badly written and badly printed" (p. 56). In his opinion, parents and teachers were obliged to "break the 'comic' magazine," and he identified the antidote: it was necessary, North argued, to ensure that young readers had recourse to quality literature. "The classics," he wrote, "are full of humor and adventure— plus good writing" (p. 56). Parents and teachers who neglected to substitute traditional literature in place of comic books were, in his opinion, "guilty of criminal negligence" (p. 56). That the newspaper reportedly received over twenty-five million requests to reprint North's editorial is evidence of the extent to which his call-to-action resonated with the public (Nyberg, 1998).

Although the outcry over comic books dissipated in the face of World War II, professional and scholarly publications aimed at teachers and librarians continued to debate the influence they had on the literary habits of developing readers. Although there were educators who insisted that comic books were detrimental to reading, there were others who acknowledged the value students attached to them and advocated a more tolerant approach. One article, written by a high school English teacher and published in *English Journal* in 1946, is of particular interest, given the theme of this journal issue. Entitled "Comic Books—A Challenge to the English Teacher," it opened by foregrounding a challenge its author felt "new" media posed for literacy educators:

> The teaching of English today is a far more complex matter than it was thirty or forty years ago. It is not that the essential character of the adolescent student has changed, or that the principles of grammar or the tenets that govern good literature have been greatly modified, but rather that the average student of the present is being molded in many ways by three potent influences: the movies, the radio, and the comic book. (Dias, 1946, p. 142)

Rather than condemn comic books as a pernicious influence, he instead chose to appropriate them as a tool with which to foster student interest in traditional literature. Characterizing his efforts to do so as "missionary work among [his] comic-book heathens," he explained how he engaged students in conversation, regarding the comic books they read with the intention of identifying a genre that appealed to them (Dias, 1946, p. 143). Having done so, he recommended a traditional work of literature he thought might interest them. This approach, he argued, made it possible for him to build on students' interests and use comic books "constructively as a stepping stone to a lasting interest in good literature" (p. 142).

Others took a similar tack. In 1942, Harriet Lee, who taught freshman English, observed that while teachers recognized a need to encourage students to evaluate their experiences with film and radio, they ignored comic books. Citing the success she experienced teaching a series of units that challenged students to critically assess the literary merit of their favorite comic books and comic strips—an approach that bears a faint resemblance to critical media literacy—she encouraged others to do the same. Two years later, W. W. D. Sones (1944), a professor of education at the University of Pittsburgh, foregrounded the instructional value of comic books and cited research that suggested they could be used to support "slow" readers and motivate "non-academic" students (p. 234), a population whose alleged lack of interest in school-based reading and writing appears to have established them as forerunners to the so-called "reluctant" reader of today. Having identified other ends toward which comic books lent themselves, Sones characterized them as vehicles with which "to realize the purposes of the school in the improvement of reading, language development, or acquisition of information" (p. 238).

Significantly, these educators were united by a shared belief—although they advocated using comic books for instructional purposes, they showed little regard for their aesthetic value. Indeed, much like those who criticized comic books, they were unable to recognize any degree of literary merit in them at all. Instead, they regarded them as a way station on a journey whose ultimate purpose was to lead students to transact with traditional literature. Comic books were, as one English teacher put it, "a stepping stone to the realms of good literature—the literature that is the necessary and rightful heritage of the adolescent" (Dias, 1946, p. 143).

It is not hard to recognize points of overlap between the arguments outlined above and those made for using graphic novels in the classroom today. By foregrounding these parallels, I do not mean to suggest that contemporary educators are entirely blind to the graphic novel's literary merit. Anyone who attends conferences or reads professional journals knows that certain titles—*Maus* (Spiegelman, 1996) and *Persepolis* (Satrapi, 2003) come readily to mind—are frequently cited as warranting close study. Nevertheless, arguments that foreground graphic novels as tools with which to support struggling readers, promote multiple literacies, motivate reluctant readers, or lead students to transact with more traditional forms of literature have the unintended effect of relegating them to a secondary role in the classroom; in doing so, they overlook the aesthetic value in much the same way as educators did in the past.

There is a difference between acknowledging (or, better yet, appropriating) a form of text and putting it to work in the classroom, and embracing it as a worthwhile form of reading material in its own right. At the current time, anecdotal evidence suggests that educators remain skeptical of the graphic novel's literary merit. Hillary Chute (2008), for example, points to "the negative reaction many in the academy have to the notion of 'literary' comics as objects of inquiry" (p. 460). Kimberly Campbell (2007), who taught middle and high school language arts prior to teaching college, recalls conversations with colleagues who expressed their "concern that graphic novels don't provide the rigor that novels require" (p. 207). I have spoken to high school teachers who were unwilling to use graphic novels with students in honors classes because they feared the ramifications. Asked to provide a rationale for teaching traditional literature—young adult or canonical—educators routinely cite its ability to foster self-reflection, initiate social change, promote tolerance, and stimulate the imagination. As those who read them know, *good graphic novels are capable of realizing these same ends.* As one junior in high school explained, "I love everything about them. I feel that they're a beautiful painting mixed with an entertaining and thought-provoking novel. They're the best of both worlds to me."

That educators should continue to question the literary merit of graphic novels is understandable. Graphic novels, like other novels, are not "value-free" texts, though we often seem to treat them as such. They have a history, and the stigmas that trail in their wake are capable of shaping our perceptions of them as a form of reading material. As John Berger (1972) observed, "The way we see things is affected by what we know or what we believe" (p. 8). Acknowledging this, a decision to introduce graphic novels in a context that has traditionally privileged "high art" can seem radical. Those who write about graphic novels, myself included, consequently recognize a need to persuade teachers—as well as parents—of their value. Yet whereas we acknowledge that teachers may question the graphic novel's literary merit, we often seem to proceed under an assumption that students will embrace them unquestioningly, as if they were somehow impervious to the stigmas their elders recognize. My experiences working with students, both at the university and high school levels, suggest that teachers who are interested in using graphic novels may expect to encounter a certain degree of resistance.

To support this assertion, allow me to share a personal anecdote. For the past three years, I taught an introductory course on young adult literature for undergraduates interested in pursuing a career in elementary or secondary education. One of the course assignments required them to compose three critical response papers in which they responded to works of literature they read over the course of the quarter. Two of the papers asked them to address traditional young adult novels, while the third invited them to respond to a graphic novel. While there were inevitably students who appreciated the opportunity to read a graphic novel, a surprisingly large number were critical of them. This was especially true of those who wished to teach high school. While they were willing to entertain the notion that young adult literature might warrant a place in the curriculum, they vehemently resisted the possibility that graphic novels might be of value as well. One student wrote:

> It's understandable to have pictures in elementary grade level books because children at that grade level are still learning about comprehension and formulation of their own ideas. Young adults are at an age where they are able (and teachers want them to) form their own ideas and think critically about books. I believe that providing pictures strips away the young adult's creative and critical thinking about books.

Another explained:

> The combination of pictures and text in novels, to me, seems childish and doesn't allow readers to think critically.

Still another student wrote:

> For my teaching goals, I want to include literature that will do at least one of three things—preferably all of them at once: encourage students to read, teach something, and broaden the reader's world view and encourage critical thinking. I do not believe that graphic novels do these things. First, there simply is not enough text to make me believe that it significantly encourages reading.

These are not extreme cases. Rather, I selected these excerpts because they are representative of the arguments I received from students who questioned the propriety of teaching graphic novels, particularly as a form of literature. It is interesting to note the negative manner in which they regarded the image, which they assumed precluded critical thinking. This is not the sort of response one might expect from members of a so-called "visual generation." Yet conversations with colleagues at professional conferences indicate that this sort of resistance to graphic novels is not uncommon.

In conducting a study designed to understand how high school students responded to multimodal texts, Hammond (2009) found that the participants with whom she worked were cognizant of a stigma attached to reading graphic novels, the result of which detracted from their popularity (p. 126). My experiences working with six sophomores and juniors who participated in a case study that sought to understand how high school students read and talk about graphic novels yielded a similar finding. A recurring theme suggested that the students were aware of stigmas attached to graphic novels; one regarded them as a puerile form of reading material, and another saw those who read them as social misfits—or, to borrow their term, "nerds."

These were not abstract arguments for one of the students, who took great pleasure in reading comic books and graphic novels. A junior in high school, Barry was familiar with the emotional pain such stigmas can cause, and when he talked about them, an underlying sense of anger often permeated his words. Reflecting on the ease with which his peers dismissed a form of reading material he valued, he wrote:

> Why should I feel ashamed when I'm at track practice calling my pals to go to the comic book store while my teammates are around, [sic] It's just strange how they can look at something that I find so beautiful, and spit on it without giving a second thought.

On another occasion, he suggested that the perception that graphic novels constituted a childish form of reading material was so prevalent, it dissuaded younger audiences from reading them, a fact he found ironic. "It's to the point now where even kids that read comics are persecuted by other kids," he explained.

It is worth noting that the students with whom I worked did not harbor a negative view of graphic novels. They volunteered to take part in an after-school reading group devoted to them, and in doing so, they evinced a willingness to explore a form of reading material that was new to some of them. That said, their cognizance of stigmas associated with graphic novels, coupled with the experience of the student who felt the disdain of his peers, suggest that these stigmas may constitute obstacles for teachers who choose to incorporate these texts into the curriculum.

In short, we cannot, as educators, proceed from a belief that students will auto-matically embrace a form of reading material that has historically been stigmatized, especially when we ask them to interact with it in a classroom context. To become a member of what Rabinowitz (1987/1998) calls a text's authorial audience, one might assume that readers have first to regard it as a viable form of reading mate-rial, a supposition that, in the case of graphic novels, may not always hold.

SO WHAT NOW?

By challenging assumptions that underlie arguments for using graphic novels, I do not wish to detract from their value. Rather, I wish to suggest that it's possible to view graphic novels in another light, one that acknowledges them as a viable font of literature that warrants close examination in its own right. My experiences working with the high school students who participated in my study consistently suggested that graphic novels are capable of inspiring high-level thinking, of stimu-lating rich discussion, and of fostering aesthetic appreciation—an observation the students shared. Sarah, a sophomore, explained:

> I think all of us have taken away just as much from like our graphic novel reading ex-perience as we have from our classroom reading experience. Maybe more. And I think . . . there's just as much substance to graphic novels as there is to just regular literature, and I don't think teachers realize that.

Another student remarked, "I didn't know they were going to have such a big impact on how I look at things in the world." Is this not the sort of thing we want students to say about their experiences with literature—indeed, about their experi-ences with art?

Good graphic novels, like good literature, are capable of moving readers to re-flect on unexamined aspects of their lives. Not all graphic novels will, of course, but the same might be said of much of the traditional literature on bookstore shelves. To increase awareness of their literary merit and to gauge their potential complexity, it is necessary for professional and scholarly journals such as this one to call for articles that subject them to the same degree of critical scrutiny afforded traditional literature. Moreover, there is a need for reviews that acknowledge titles beyond the usual standards and that help educators keep pace with the multitude of graphic novels published each year. Finally, there is a need for a field-wide con-versation that identifies the challenges involved in using graphic novels so that we might begin to address them and, in doing so, develop a sense of appreciation for their artistic merit.

SEAN CONNORS *is an assistant professor of English Education in the Department of Curriculum and Instruction, College of Education and Health Professions, at the Uni-versity of Arkansas, Fayetteville. Prior to pursuing his doctoral degree, Sean taught English at Coconino High School in Flagstaff, Arizona. He has taught undergraduate courses in Young Adult Literature, as well as an English Education Lab Experience course for potential preservice English language arts teachers. His scholarly interests include understanding how adolescents read and experience graphic novels, and asking how educators might expand the use of diverse critical perspectives in secondary school literature curricula. When he isn't reading graphic novels and young adult literature, Sean enjoys hiking with his wife and dogs and rooting for the Red Sox.*

WORKS CITED

Berger, J. (1972). *Ways of seeing.* New York: Viking Press.

Bitz, M. (2004). The comic book project: Forging alternative pathways to literacy. *Journal of Adolescent & Adult Literacy, 47,* 574–586.

Campbell, K. H. (2007). *Less is more: Teaching literature with short texts—grades 6–12.* Portland, ME: Stenhouse.

Chute, H. (2008). Comics as literature? Reading graphic narrative. *Publications of the Modern Language Association of America, 123,* 452–465.

Crawford, P. (2004). A novel approach: Using graphic novels to attract reluctant readers and promote literacy. *Library Media Connection, 22*(5), 26–28.

Dias, E. J. (1946). Comic books—A challenge to the English teacher. *English Journal, 35*(3), 142–145.

Dorrell, L. D. Why comic books? *School Library Journal, 34*(3), 30–32.

Eisner, W. (1985). *Comics and sequential art: Principles & practice of the world's most popular art form.* Tamarac, FL: Poorhouse Press.

Frey, N., & Fisher, D. (2008). *Teaching visual literacy: Using comic books, graphic novels, anime, cartoons, and more to develop comprehension and thinking skills.* Thousand Oaks, CA: Corwin Press.

Frey, N., & Fisher, D. (2004). Using graphic novels, anime, and the Internet in an urban high school. *English Journal, 93*(3), 19–25.

Hajdu, D. (2008). *The ten-cent plague: The great comic-book scare and how it changed America.* New York: Picador.

Hammond, H. K. (2009). *Graphic novels and multimodal literacy: A reader response study.* Unpublished doctoral dissertation, University of Minnesota.

Lee, H. E. (1942). Discrimination in reading. *English Journal, 3 7*(9), 677–679.

Morrison, T. G., Bryan, G., & Chilcoat, G. W. (2002). Using student-generated comic books in the classroom. *Journal of Adolescent & Adult Literacy, 45,* 758–767.

North, S. (1940, June). A national disgrace. *Illinois Libraries*, p. 3.

Nyberg, A. K. (1998). *Seal of approval: The history of the comics code*. Jackson, MS: University Press of Mississippi.

Rabinowitz, P. J. (1987/1998). *Before reading: Narrative conventions and the politics of interpretation*. Columbus: Ohio State University Press.

Ranker, J. (2007). Using comic books as read-alouds: Insights on reading instruction from an English as a second language classroom. *The Reading Teacher*, 61, 296–305.

Satrapi, M. (2003). *Persepolis: The story of a childhood*. New York: Pantheon.

Sones, W. W. D. (1944). The comics and the instructional method. *Journal of Educational Sociology*, 18, 232–240.

Spiegelman, A (1996). *The complete Maus: A survivor's tale*. New York: Pantheon.

Expanding Literacies through Graphic Novels[*]

By Gretchen Schwarz
English Journal, July 2006

> Time has arrived to broaden the canons of traditional education and the curriculum. . . .
> Using critical pedagogy to integrate the new forms of visual and electronic
> "texts" represents a curriculum requiring new competencies and a new definition
> of what constitutes learning as well as how and when it takes place.
> —*Laudislaus M. Semali*, Literacy in Multimedia America

The graphic novel now offers English language arts teachers opportunities to engage all students in a medium that expands beyond the traditional borders of literacy. The *graphic novel*, a longer and more artful version of the comic book bound as a "real" book, is increasingly popular, available, and meaningful. Library media specialists have been in the forefront advocating graphic novels. For example, Maureen Mooney declares, "If you acquire graphic novels, young adults will come." Mooney adds that graphic novels appeal to various readers, offer all kinds of genres, help students develop critical thinking, and encourage literacy (18). Literary critics are also taking note. Lev Grossman observes, "Yet some of the most interesting, most daring, most heartbreaking art being created right now, of both the verbal and visual varieties, is being published in graphic novels. These books take on memory, alienation, film noir, child abuse, life in post-revolutionary Iran and, of course, love" (56). In addition, *Standards for the English Language Arts* promotes a wide variety of texts, "print and nonprint," facility with "visual language," and participation in a "variety of literacy communities" (NCTE and IRA 3). The time has come for secondary English teachers to explore and use the graphic novel to build multiple literacies.

First, the graphic novel is helpful in promoting the goals of traditional literacy. Getting students reading is one benefit, as literacy expert Stephen D. Krashen argues in his latest edition of *The Power of Reading: Insights from the Research*. Educators have also urged the use of comics as an alternative, appealing way for students to analyze literary conventions, character development, dialogue, satire, and lan-

---

guage structures as well as develop writing and research skills. Rocco Versaci maintains that graphic novels can "increase and some of the most interesting, diversify the voices that our students experience in the classroom and suggest to them that literature may take various forms" (66). Such study can even encourage students to question the notions of the canon. Timothy G. Morrison, Gregory Bryan, and George W. Chilcoat describe how creating graphic novels in class can help middle school students "develop their writing, comprehension, and research skills in a cross-curricular activity" (759). Phyllis Hartfiel, a mid-high teacher from northeastern Oklahoma, includes the graphic novel in her study of *Romeo and Juliet*. Hartfiel has her ninth-grade students create a graphic-novel version of the play that allows them to communicate what they thought most important and that serves as a good review. Hartfiel thinks that this playful approach to Shakespeare requires students to solve problems and make decisions about such literary elements as narrative style and character presentation. The students also create a rubric for evaluating the graphic novels they produce, under the teacher's direction, requiring further critical thinking.

Even at the college level, Martin Wallen, an English professor at a major state university in Oklahoma, has used the graphic novel *From Hell* by Alan Moore and Eddie Campbell in a popular-fiction course based on Jack the Ripper literature. He chose the book not because it was any graphic novel but because it is one of the best and fit the course topic. Wallen noted that *From Hell* "takes the lurid sensationalism that has always surrounded the Ripper murders and turns it into a self-conscious commentary on our fascination with violence and lurid sensationalism . . . . It enabled us to talk about the exploitative aspects of sensational literature and cinema." His college students responded well, and *From Hell* is not an easy book to read. Not only is the story long and sometimes confusing, with flashbacks, hallucinations, and visions of the future, but the research footnotes in Appendix I run forty-two pages. Moreover, the black-and-white drawings capture the somber setting of lower-class London at the time of Jack the Ripper, and the violence and sex are fairly graphic (not appropriate for younger students). *From Hell* is a well-told and disturbing, thought-provoking work, what any English teacher would want from any work of literature. Traditional aims can be served by using the graphic novel in the classroom; the graphic novel can be legitimate literature.

Increasingly, scholars and teachers realize that in a media-dominated society, one traditional literacy—reading and writing of print—is no longer sufficient. Today's young people also have to read films, TV shows, magazines, and Web sites. Both practical information and the stories of our culture come from many media, especially those made possible by current technology. Donna E. Alvermann and Margaret C. Hagood argue, "As a result of the greater demands that students face in New Times, they must acquire the analytic tools necessary for critically 'reading' all kinds of media texts—film, video, MTV, the Internet, and so on; hence, our interest in incorporating critical media literacy in school curricula" (203). Both traditional, alphabetic literacy and literacies such as information, visual, and media literacy can be well served by classroom engagement with the graphic novel.

The graphic novel is a medium that combines the visual and verbal as do films, TV, and even pop-up ads. The graphic novel, however, holds still and allows special attention to be given to its unique visual and word arrangement. As Robin Varnum and Christina T. Gibbons declare in *The Language of Comics: Word and Image*, "There is a synergy between words and pictures in comics such that their combined effect is greater than or different from what might have been predicted" (xiv). To read and interpret graphic novels, students have to pay attention to the usual literary elements of character, plot, and dialogue, and they also have to consider visual elements such as color, shading, panel layout, perspective, and even the lettering style. For example, I shared the short story "Hurdles," from a graphic novel collection by Derek Kirk Kim (available online at http://lowbright.com/Comics/ Hurdles/ Hurdles.htm), with a group of adults in the Language, Literacy, and Culture doctoral seminar. The discussion of this short piece revealed the complexity and sophistication of this literary medium.

Kim's "Hurdles" is, some students claimed, a poem. In fact, the way the words are laid out on the page next to the pictures rather than in the usual speech balloons, the rhythm of the narrative, and even the repetition of the first and last sentences add to the poetic quality of this short piece. Other elements also come into play. The black-and-white artwork and the title "Hurdles" styled as hurdles on a race course add to the serious tone. The perspective is telling. The school boys are just running legs in one panel, and the protagonist is looking up to the coach in the third-to-last panel. The coach has great power over these adolescents. The coach himself is just a pair of sunglasses on a nose, holding still, closed off. He is not portrayed as a fully human figure, and his ignorant racism is reflected in his stance. Of course, the hurdles as physical barriers also become the symbolic barrier of prejudice for the boy. Much more could be discovered and discussed in this piece; its effect is visceral, through the combination of words and pictures. As the American father of the graphic novel, Will Eisner, observes of the medium, "It is in every sense a singular form of reading" (5).

Some graphic novels, and the term includes all genres, are designed to inform and persuade. New media call for a "new rhetoric," one that includes visual as well as verbal understanding and ability, as demonstrated in *Visual Communication: A Writer's Guide* by Susan Hilligoss. This handbook, aimed at college students, acknowledges that new technologies make the *visual* design of documents significant. Hilligoss summarizes as follows: "[C]ollege students . . . prepare their work with sophisticated computers and printers that rival the output of commercial printing . . . . They have access to a wealth of graphics via the Internet and inexpensive collections of clip art, as well as the means to create digital photographs and artwork. They make pages for the World Wide Web and effectively publish their work to a large audience. . . . In short, the world of college writing has changed" (1). Younger students likewise read and create arguments and do research in ways beyond simple print. The graphic novel offers an engaging medium for asking students to analyze information and persuasion in different ways.

For example, Joel Andreas's *Addicted to War* is a graphic novel heavy on verbal text that is a manifesto aimed at American militarism. Well supported with statistics and references, *Addicted to War* combines cartoon pictures with black-and-white photographs and covers its topic from the first chapter on Manifest Destiny through the Cold War and the "War on Terror" to the last chapter, "Resisting Militarism." *Addicted to War* does not aim to give a neutral, textbook view but rather to persuade the reader that American militarism is wrong. The Korean War is mentioned on page 13 in two panels, one showing a cartoon General MacArthur boasting about American might (with obscenities indicated) as the text describes the "ambitious plans" of the US State Department to show that Western technology could defeat "any Asian army." Certain key phrases such as "ambitious plans" and "revolutions and anticolonial wars" are in bold text. The second panel shows a photograph of American soldiers fighting in a village and a cartoon skeleton saying, "Waiting for another war," while the narrative text describes the death statistics and notes that the United States did not win this war. This graphic novel is not subtle, but such a work offers a good place to begin to analyze visual along with verbal persuasion. Students should ask who the target audience for *Addicted to War* is and who is not the audience. How were the photographs chosen? How do the cartoon figures affect the reader, especially the satirical figures? How were the facts chosen and connected? What is the effect of the list of antiwar organizations at the end of the book? How does the lettering affect the reader? Other graphic novels take on current events, versions of historical events, even other media. Today's young people need the knowledge and skills to deal with persuasion in an age of images.

Finally, the graphic novel offers teachers the opportunity to implement critical media literacy in the classroom—literacy that affirms diversity, gives voice to all, and helps students examine ideas and practices that promulgate inequity. Many graphic novels offer more diverse voices than traditional textbooks and can open up discussion about issues such as social justice. For example, *The Four Immigrants Manga: A Japanese Experience in San Francisco, 1904–1924* by Henry (Yoshitaka) Kiyama, translated into English by Frederik L. Schodt, portrays the struggles of four Japanese immigrants. Manga is the Japanese term for graphic novel, and the medium has a respected history in Japan. This narrative is both funny and disturbing as the four men work hard to become successful in their new home but suffer injustices and prejudices. Interestingly, Kiyama, as Schodt observes in the introduction, does not adhere to the American convention of the time of "drawing obsequious Japanese with slanted eyes and buckteeth (later with glasses and eventually cameras added)" (16). In its narrative and in its visuals, this graphic novel is a challenge to stereotypes and a new medium for examining such concepts.

Likewise, *Still I Rise: A Cartoon History of African Americans* challenges assumptions about the poor, victim blacks, who actually accomplished much while surviving slavery and racism (Laird and Laird); this book would work well to connect the English class to history. A graphic novel such as *Dignifying Science: Stories about Women Scientists* challenges the notion that scientific discoveries have been made by all or mostly males, making it a good book to connect to science classes

(Ottaviani). The illustrations were all done by women artists. Graphic novels can not only be used for encouraging critical media literacy but also for encouraging cross-curriculum connections.

The work of one middle school teacher near Tulsa, Oklahoma, Carrie Edwards, illustrated the potential for graphic novels in celebrating diversity. Edwards brought in graphic novels as they supported her seventh-grade language arts course. For example, certain manga that are quite popular with middle school students include elements of Chinese mythology, such as warrior figures, which fit a unit on mythology. Even the form of the manga—which usually has to be read from back to front, from the American perspective—offered Edwards the opportunity to compare Japanese and American culture. Manga and other graphic novels can also offer situations to which adolescents can relate, as in *Fruits Basket*, in which one girl is a "rice ball" and does not fit. Graphic novels present issues of difference and belonging, according to Edwards, and students enjoyed reading them, discussing them, researching them online, exploring animated versions of novels, and drawing characters and scenes from these books. The manga "open up so many things," said Edwards, enabling the exploration of multiple literacies.

Using graphic novels in the classroom does present a challenge to teachers; a number of obstacles and concerns arise. First, anything new often faces resistance, especially if it is part of popular culture. Finding classroom-appropriate works is also a concern. Not all graphic novels are appropriate, and even some of the best contain profanity and sexual and violent content. Teachers will need to apprise their principals and parents of their plans and be able to offer a good rationale for using specific graphic novels in their courses. Censorship remains a problem around the country, and many educators, too, are loath to encounter any controversy in the classroom.

Second, graphic novels are not on the state or national tests. The alignment of curriculum and standardized testing is a growing problem, especially given the demands of legislation such as No Child Left Behind. Moreover, new literacies may not be widely accepted nor included in the district or school curriculum objectives. The current political climate is not particularly supportive of innovation. Even obtaining funding for graphic novels may be difficult.

Finally, teachers themselves will have to do their homework. Teachers must extend their ideas about and skills in multiple literacies; media literacy or critical literacy may not be familiar concepts. Fortunately, there are excellent works that can help teachers new to the field of graphic novels. For the beginning reader of the medium, Stephen Weiner's *The 101 Best Graphic Novels* and Michele Gorman's *Getting Graphic! Using Graphic Novels to Promote Literacy with Preteens and Teens* offer many useful titles and helpful background information. Both Weiner and Gorman are library media specialists. Much information about various titles and where they can be obtained is also available online. Second, several titles offer excellent insights into the ways graphic novels work on readers: *Understanding Comics: The Invisible Art* by Scott McCloud (in graphic novel form), *The Art of the Comic Book: An Aesthetic History* by Robert C. Harvey, and works by Will Eisner. One can also find information online from librarians, publishers, and from teenagers themselves. In addition, new books are coming out, such as *Writing and Illustrating the Graphic Novel: Everything You Need to Know to Create Great Graphic Works* by Mike Chinn, that can help teachers and their students create graphic novels as well as read them. One of the advantages of graphic novels for the teacher is their freshness, and the teacher and students must work together to make meanings and to explore multiple literacies.

Graphic novels are increasing in number, quality, variety, and availability. They offer a new kind of text for the classroom and they demand new reading abilities. They tend to appeal to diverse students, including reluctant readers, and they offer both great stories and informational topics. For students who no longer deal with pure word texts in their daily lives, multiple literacies are a necessity. Schools must prepare young people to think critically with and about all kinds of texts.

WORKS CITED

Alvermann, Donna E., and Margaret C. Hagood. "Critical Media Literacy: Research, Theory, and Practice in 'New Times.'" *The Journal of Educational Research* 93.3 (2000): 193–205.

Andreas, Joel. *Addicted to War*. Oakland: AK, 2002.

Chinn, Mike. *Writing and Illustrating the Graphic Novel: Everything You Need to Know to Create Great Graphic Works*. Hauppauge: Barron's, 2004.

Edwards, Carrie. Telephone interview. 7 Feb. 2004.

Eisner, Will. *Graphic Storytelling and Visual Narrative*. Tamarac: Poorhouse, 1996.

Gorman, Michele. *Getting Graphic! Using Graphic Novels to Promote Literacy with Preteens and Teens*. Worthington: Linworth, 2003.

Grossman, Lev. "Singing a New Toon." *Time* 162.8 (25 Aug. 2003): 56–58.

Hartfiel, Phyllis. Interview. 1 Aug. 2004.

Harvey, Robert C. *The Art of the Comic Book: An Aesthetic History*. Jackson: UP of Mississippi, 1996.

Hilligoss, Susan. *Visual Communication: A Writer's Guide*. New York: Longman, 2000.

Kim, Derek Kirk. *Same Differences and Other Stories*. Marietta: Top Shelf, 2004.

Kiyama, Henry (Yoshitaka). *The Four Immigrants Manga: A Japanese Experience in San Francisco, 1904–1924*. Trans. Frederik L. Schodt. Berkeley: Stone Bridge, 1999.

Krashen, Stephen D. *The Power of Reading: Insights from the Research*. 2nd ed. Westport: Libraries Unlimited, 2004.

Laird, Roland Owen, Jr., with Taneshia Nash Laird. *Still I Rise: A Cartoon History of African Americans*. New York: Norton, 1997.

McCloud, Scott. *Understanding Comics: The Invisible Art*. New York: Harper, 1993.

Mooney, Maureen. "Graphic Novels: How They Can Work in Libraries." *The Book Report* 21.3 (2002): 18–19.

Moore, Alan, and Eddie Campbell. *From Hell*. Paddington, Australia: Eddie Campbell Comics, 1999.

Morrison, Timothy G., Gregory Bryan, and George W. Chilcoat. "Using Student-Generated Comic Books in the Classroom." *Journal of Adolescent and Adult Literacy* 45.8 (2002): 758–67.

NCTE and IRA. *Standards for the English Language Arts*. Urbana: NCTE, 1996.

Ottaviani, Jim. *Dignifying Science: Stories about Women Scientists*. Ann Arbor: G. T. Labs, 1999.

Semali, Ladislaus M. *Literacy in Multimedia America: Integrating Media Education across the Curriculum*. New York: Falmer, 2000.

Varnum, Robin, and Christina T. Gibbons, eds. Introduction. *The Language of Comics: Word and Image*. Jackson: UP of Mississippi, 2001.

Versaci, Rocco. "How Comic Books Can Change the Way Our Students See Literature: One Teacher's Perspective." *English Journal* 91.2 (2001): 61–67.

Wallen, Martin. Online interview. 12 Mar. 2004.

Weiner, Stephen. *The 101 Best Graphic Novels*. New York: NBM, 2001.

A former high school English and German teacher, GRETCHEN SCHWARZ *now teaches curriculum studies at Oklahoma State University. Her research interests include media literacy and graphic novels. email: ges1004@okstate.edu.*

4

Graphica in the Stacks:
The Role of Librarians

Editor's Introduction

Articles in the previous chapters touch on the important role librarians have played in promoting and legitimizing graphic novels. The entries in this chapter take a closer look at their influence, examining how librarians select titles, integrate them into their collections, and educate sometimes skeptical community members about the benefits of the medium.

In "Graphic Novels for (Really) Young Readers," the first article in the chapter, elementary school media specialist Allyson A. W. Lyga offers tips on how to select and use age-appropriate graphic novels. She discusses selling parents and colleagues on the merits of graphic novels and shares teaching exercises she's found to be successful. In defending the form, Lyga says graphic novels, by virtue of telling stories and developing characters with both words and pictures, "give the brain more of a workout per sentence than any other type of media, including conventional books." Lyga even sings the praises of wordless graphic novels, crediting *Owly*, one such comic, with teaching one of her third graders a host of critical skills. Lyga ends the piece with a list of recommended titles, breaking them down by genre.

In the chapter's next entry, John Hogan's roundtable discussion "Graphic Novels in Today's Libraries," four librarians from across the United States talk about how they select and shelve graphic novels, maintain their collections, and overcome space issues, budgetary constraints, and other challenges. Since graphic novels are created for children and adults alike, the librarians explain how they differentiate between titles appropriate for different age groups. Some comic companies provide their own age ratings, but according to Eva Volin, a children's librarian in Alameda, California, the industry lacks a consistent rating system, such as the one used by the Motion Picture Association of America (MPAA).

In "Reinventing the Book Club: Graphic Novels as Educational Heavyweights," librarian Jonathan Seyfried recalls the excitement and enthusiasm generated by the graphic-novel book club he started at his San Francisco middle school. Seyfried summarizes the semester-long elective, talks about the graphic novels his students read and discussed, and lists tips on choosing comics for schools. "My students crave stories that they can relate to, written in a language they can understand, with jokes they can get, and metaphors that are clear to them," Seyfried writes.

With "Graphic Novels and School Libraries," the subsequent entry in this chapter, Hollis Margaret Rudiger and Megan Schliesman give helpful advice for librarians on how to select, catalog, and teach graphic novels in school libraries. They also cite the importance of following collection-development policies, which guide librarians in meeting the needs of their communities, and explore the question of whether to shelve all graphic novels together or spread them out according to subject. Many librarians prefer the former method, as it "creates a focal point for readers who might not be regular users of the library but are drawn in by graphic novel collections," according to the authors.

Graphic Novels for (Really) Young Readers[*]

By Allyson A. W. Lyga
School Library Journal, March 1, 2006

Since I started stocking our school library with graphic novels six years ago, I've discovered that kids love them. Our collection, for students in kindergarten through fifth grade, now has around 125 graphic novels, and they're by far our most heavily circulated items. Every year, I add about 20 to 25 new ones, and I'm convinced that the time and money I've invested in those titles have been my best collection development decision to date.

Of course not everyone thinks graphic novels are wonderful. Some teachers, parents, and even media specialists wonder if they're even appropriate for young students to read. Are graphic novels really worth purchasing? Or do they just pander to kids' wants without meeting their educational needs? To best answer those questions, let me share a typical experience I had with one of our third graders, a below-average reader named Bryonna.

Bryonna checked out a copy of *Owly*, one of our most popular graphic novels, earlier in the year. She came up to me before class and held it up: "I love this book," she said. "It's my favorite book!" I was thrilled and wanted to know more. "It's a story about friendship, and there aren't any words in the book," she told me. "I read the story to my two-year-old sister, and she loved it, too!" "How did you read a book without words?" I asked her. Bryonna explained that when she looked at the pictures she thought about the words the characters were saying and she visualized the words in her head. Then, when she read the story to her sister, she created the dialogue and story based on the pictures.

For a young child to read a graphic novel, much less a wordless one, many essential literacy skills are required, including the ability to understand a sequence of events, interpret characters' nonverbal gestures, discern the story's plot, and make inferences. Best of all, these skills don't merely apply to *Owly* or to graphic novels. They are the critical skills that govern *all* reading comprehension, making Bryonna's triumph with *Owly* into a lesson that has also helped her with other reading materials.

BRAIN FOOD

I always like to say that, educationally speaking, graphic novels give the brain more of a workout per sentence than any other type of media, including conventional books. That's because as a reader takes in a graphic novel's print and art through a series of panels, word balloons, and captions, the reader's brain is bombarded simultaneously with the graphic novel's characters, setting, plot, and action. So if a parent or teacher claims that reading graphic novels isn't much of a challenge for a child, hand him one. Explain how the brain works to comprehend the story and how it detects the subtle nuances of the characters' facial expressions.

Graphic novels help all different types of learners. For children who are incapable of visualizing a story, the artwork helps them create context. Graphic elements also attract visually dependent readers, who then freely read the text, and help reluctant readers (or as I like to call them, "avoidance readers") understand the plot of a story. Finally, graphic novels cross gender lines. Boys always gravitate toward my graphic novel collection—they are often picture-driven creatures who like our fantasy, action, and adventure titles such as *Bone*, *X-Men*, *Superman*, *Adventures of Tintin*, and *Buzzboy*. On the other hand, girls are attracted to graphic novels that relate to their interest in forming friendships, such as *Peanutbutter and Jeremy's Best Book Ever* and *Monkey vs. Robot*. Instead of forcing my students to alter their interests, I treat them as individuals with varying tastes and our collection caters to them.

GENTLE PERSUASION

There are certain steps you can take to convince a skeptical colleague or an unsupportive parent to see the merits of graphic novels. Examine some graphic novels so that any objectionable artwork or mature plot lines can be avoided. For example, I never purchase graphic novels about war or crime, because many of them are too violent for young children. And of course if something is R-rated, I'm not about to put it in my elementary school collection.

Unlike ordering traditional nonfiction and fiction titles, where you head straight to review sources, book jobbers, and catalogs, visit a comic-book store and talk with the owner or an employee about your students and the community you teach in. For example, what are the ages of your students? Is your community conservative or is it open-minded? Bring along a list of curricular topics, recreational reading topics, and your students' favorite television shows so that the owner has a better idea of what to suggest for your collection. By matching graphic novels with your school's curriculum, you'll be able to offer teachers new titles instead of their "old faithful."

This happened to a third-grade teacher when she came to check out materials for a unit on folk and fairy tales. I surprised her with Patrick Atangan's *The Yellow Jar*, a perfect retelling of two old Japanese folktales with the art drawn in traditional *ukiyo-e* or woodblock style. Instead of simply teaching her students about the story—like she usually did—*The Yellow Jar* enabled her to show them how to critically analyze the art that accompanied it. The students were able to see how the art reflected the culture and how it was used to tell the story.

Many children's television shows are branching out into cine-manga, basically a Japanese-style graphic novel with actual film shots incorporated into the book. They are glossy, soft-cover books that are extremely popular with children. Disney's *Lizzie McGuire* and TokyoPop's *SpongeBob SquarePants* are two examples in my collection. This is a perfect way to get reluctant readers to read because it connects interest in their favorite TV shows with literacy. It's also a perfect way to get more teachers to visit the media center. Many of our teachers have used these books in their classrooms and report that they've been very successful in getting children to read them for pleasure. Now, instead of students writing book reports about their favorite novels, they're writing about their favorite *graphic* novels. In fact, some of these reports have been created as graphic novels themselves!

You'll also want to pay close attention to the artwork in the graphic novels you're purchasing, as this is an area of concern for many teachers and parents. Some artwork might be too mature or inappropriate for elementary school students. With graphic novels, everything is on display and there can be no question as to what the student is viewing. Therefore, the art as well as the story line must be carefully scrutinized.

Make sure to inquire about upcoming titles and series. Store owners get catalogs and press releases, so if you like a certain author or type of story, ask about upcoming issues or if there are any "crossover" stories your students might enjoy. Crossover stories, such as *JLA: The Ultimate Guide to the Justice League of America*, are ones in which an established character visits different settings and experiences unusual adventures. A little time spent examining graphic novels before you purchase them will prevent future problems. Meanwhile, you have made a new friend in a comic-book store retailer.

THINK SMALL

DC and Marvel are two of the most familiar names in comics. Sure, they produce the most popular superheroes around: Batman, Superman, Spider-Man, and X-Men. Superhero comics are wonderful but some story lines are darker and more mature than others. Based on these dark story lines, some parents and teachers believe that all graphic novels contain inappropriate material for children, but this is simply not true. There are many graphic novels suitable for what I call "the little guys"—those second to fifth graders who are becoming confident independent readers. I only purchase developmentally appropriate titles for my students and many of them are suitable for all ages. Many of these precious stories are written and published by smaller presses, like Top Shelf and NBM, which released *The Yellow Jar*. Some are even self-published, which makes these graphic novels more difficult to find because major distributors or book jobbers don't solicit them. In this case, the trip to the comic-book store to find graphic novels by smaller presses could make a difference in what you add to your collection. Without my visits, I would not have had *Owly* for my student Bryonna or *The Yellow Jar* for a teacher.

For a unique professional development experience, visit comic-book conventions to meet authors and illustrators firsthand and to check out the suitability of their stories for your community and age level. I attended the 2005 Baltimore ComicCon and discovered some gems: *Banana Tail*, *Bumperboy*, and *Salamander Dream*. While there, artist and author Andy Runton signed copies of *Owly* for my school. He was thrilled that elementary students have been enjoying his small-press book, and he showed me the prototype of the plush Owly that his mother sewed.

IMPROVE READING COMPREHENSION

Along with our reading specialist, I've used graphic novels to create reading comprehension lessons for a group of struggling fourth-grade boys. The typical classroom methods of using scaffolding, word lists, and graphic organizers weren't helping them become better readers or enjoy the reading experience.

Using a wordless graphic novel called *Li'l Santa*, students were encouraged to unlock the plot's meaning through pictures and the subtle details and nuances of the characters' facial expressions. Since these students love TV programs, movies, and video games, I knew that they could handle the task and enjoy the process.

While examining the graphics, they used Post-it notes to dictate to us their ideas for dialog and captions. They liked sticking the notes directly onto the page, which also bookmarked where they left off at the end of each class. Using their notes, students transcribed their stories onto sheets of paper—with each numbered page corresponding to a scene in the book. In other words, students literally wrote the story and thus demonstrated that they understood the graphic novel. When we showed the boys' work to their classroom teachers, they were amazed by the students' word choices and dialog—and by their deep understanding of what they had read.

GROW YOUR OWN

Another great way to promote literacy is for students to create their own graphic novels. With their classroom teacher, students can use graphic organizers to plan their tales using all of the story elements: characterization, setting, plot, action, problem, and resolution. By working in pairs, students can capitalize on each other's writing and artistic strengths. Next, in my media class, I went over the format of a graphic novel—panels, gutters, word balloons, and captions. We discussed the importance of the flow of the story from one panel to the next and examined some models.

Then students made some rough sketches, which they brought along to art class. The art teacher taught them how to add depth and movement to their images with ink and dark pencils. Over the course of a few art periods, students finished their creations and gained a better appreciation of the process and the teamwork required to make graphic novels. This activity was literacy in action—students were actively involved in every step, becoming their own readers and critics.

FAIR TRADE

Penny Foster, a media specialist at Century High School in Maryland, has the ultimate idea with graphic novels. She worked with Diamond Comic Distributors, a graphic-novel book distributor, to set up a graphic-novel book fair to raise money for the school library. The fair included a book signing by a graphic novelist, graphic novels for elementary and middle school students, and a display of this genre made by high school students. The fair offered local families a unique experience, bringing together elementary, middle school, and high school students and their parents and showcasing literacy through the arts.

GRAPHIC NOVELS ALL AROUND!

I've seen my boys' recreational reading habits bloom because they're requesting graphic novels, and I've witnessed the most non-avid readers become active book promoters. Even my nonverbal students are talking about what graphic novels they're reading.

I'm able to share these positive changes with classroom teachers, which may seem trivial on the surface, but is actually an important part of collaborating with colleagues and helping students. When a teacher is trying to motivate a child to learn or a speech teacher is stumped, the behavior and attitudes that I can observe and relate become invaluable: Teachers can encourage students to write a report based on the graphic novel title. Speech teachers can assist students in talking about the characters and plot in graphic novels.

As librarians, we know that enthusiasm for reading often wanes as children get older, so it's a shock and a delight to see a group of fifth-grade boys running to the shelves to recommend titles to their friends . . . and then booktalk titles and reserve graphic novels to read after their friends have devoured them! Yes, simple "happy talk" about graphic novels may seem inconsequential but it indicates enthusiasm and a confident reader who will be ready for more challenging material.

THANKS, MRS. L.

Some interesting things have happened to me since I included graphic novels in my collection. I've had a grandfather hug me for having *Golden Age Superman* in my library. His grandson brought the book with him during a visit and upon opening the book, the grandfather saw the *Superman* comics of his childhood days. He told me that he felt even closer to his grandson because he was reading what he enjoyed as a child. I was astonished but happy that graphic novels had bridged the intergenerational gap.

I had a pastor thank me for having comic books and graphic novels because his son brought them home and read them cover-to-cover. Seeing his son read them reminded him of what he enjoyed reading as a teenager—comic books. The two now enjoy weekly visits together to the comic-book store.

Best yet, I've seen countless students like Bryonna, the struggling third grader, who are well on their way to becoming successful readers—thanks to graphic novels.

WHAT LITTLE KIDS LOVE

ACTION AND ADVENTURE

Hergé. *The Adventures of Tintin: Volume 1.* illus. by author. tr. by Leslie Lonsdale-Cooper & Michael Turner. Little, Brown. 1994. Tr $18.99. ISBN 0-316-35940-8.
Gr 4–6—Children will love tagging along on the adventures of this young roving reporter and his precious dog, Snowy. The highly detailed descriptions of international sites will make the places come alive and transport young readers around the world.

Kochalka, James. *Pinky & Stinky.* illus. by author. Top Shelf. 2002. pap. $17.95. ISBN 1-89183-029-5.
Gr 3–5—In this typical good versus evil tale, two astronaut pigs want to search the moon but their plans are foiled by some human astronauts. A great story to spur conversations about pursuing one's talents and how others may try to stop individuals from reaching their potential.

Torres, J. *The Collected Alison Dare: Little Miss Adventures.* 2002. $8.95. ISBN 1-92999-820-1.

——. *The Collected Alison Dare: Little Miss Adventures Volume 2.* 2005. $11.95. ISBN 1-93266-425-4. ea vol: illus. by J. Bone. Oni. pap.
Gr 4–5—Her archaeologist mother and superhero father allow Alison to get whatever she wants, even if it means zapping her friends from their homes to wherever she happens to be in the world! In the second book, the young heroine and her boarding school friends battle the Blue Scarab and go on museum adventures with mom.

HUMOR

Davis, John. *The Adventures of Jimmy Neutron Boy Genius: Tinkering with Destiny*. illus. TokyoPop. 2003. pap. $1.25. ISBN 1-59182-401-X.
Gr 4–5—Packed with the same action and adventure as the animated TV show, this cine-manga-style book will attract fans of the series. All of the illustrations are screen shots or cells used in the making of the popular cartoon.

Gaiman, Neil. The *Day I Swapped My Dad for Two Goldfish*. illus. by Dave McKean. HarperCollins. 2004. Tr $16.99. ISBN 0-06-058701-6.
Gr 3–5—In this aptly titled, humorous book, a child desires a pet goldfish and is willing do anything to achieve this goal.

Hillenburg, Stephen. *SpongeBob SquarePants: Crime and Funishment*. illus. TokyoPop. 2004. pap. $7.99. ISBN 1-59182-576-8.
Gr 3–5—This cine-manga adaptation of the extremely popular children's television show is a great selection for students who enjoy watching SpongeBob and his crazy, ocean-dwelling friends on TV.

Huey, Debbie. *Bumperboy Loses His Marbles!* illus. by author. Adhouse. 2005. pap. $7.95. ISBN 0-976-66100-4.
Gr 2–4—Bumperboy of Bubtopia wants to compete in the big marble championship but has lost all of his precious tiny balls. To make matters worse, his lucky marble is in the hands of his enemy.

Kochalka, James. *Peanutbutter & Jeremy's Best Book Ever!* illus. by author. Alternative Comics. 2003. pap. $14.95. ISBN 1-89186-746-6.
Gr 4–5—Peanutbutter the cat and Jeremy the crow are the stars in this amusing tale of friendship filled with silly tricks. The format, a collection of short stories, will empower children to finish this "thick book."

Peterson, Scott. *Disney Classic Cartoon Tales*. illus. Disney. 2005. Tr $14.99. ISBN 0-7868-3517-6.
Gr 2–5—Children will be familiar with the characters in this collection of short stories but they will find all new plots to keep them entertained.

FANTASY

Burton, Tim. *Tim Burton's the Nightmare Before Christmas*. illus. Disney. 2005. pap. $8.99. ISBN 0-7868-3849-3.
Gr 4–5—Students will enjoy this manga version of the popular movie. The artwork will transport them right back to Halloweentown and to the plot to ruin Christmas by kidnapping Santa.

Larson, Hope. *Salamander Dream*. illus. by author. AdHouse. 2005. pap. $15. ISBN 0-972-17949-6.

Gr 4–6—Over many years, Hailey goes into the magical woods and shares her beliefs in magic and hope with a girl she meets named Salamander. Each summer, the girls take turns telling stories, which in turn, follow Hailey's development from a child to a young woman.

Smith, Jeff. *Bone: Out from Boneville*. illus. by author. Graphix. 2005. Tr $18.95. ISBN 0-439-70623-8.

Gr 4 Up—This witty tale of friendship and adventure, republished with full-color illustrations by Scholastic's graphic novel imprint, is a perfect book for all ages.

FOLKTALES

Atangan, Patrick. *The Yellow Jar: Volume I: Two Tales from Japanese Tradition*. illus. by author. NBM. 2002. Tr $12.95. ISBN 1-56163-331-3.

Gr 5 Up—Done in the traditional Japanese woodblock style, this beautiful adaptation of two folktales is so well done that it could be used in art class to model Japanese drawing techniques.

FRIENDSHIP STORIES

Gownley, Jimmy. *Amelia Rules! The Whole World's Crazy*. 2005. ISBN 1-59687-819-3.

——. *Amelia Rules!: What Makes You Happy*. 2004. ISBN 0-7434-7909-2. ea vol: illus. by author. ibooks. pap. $14.95.

Gr 3–5—Fourth-grader Amelia has a crazy life living with her recently divorced mother and Aunt Tanner. She also has some nutty friends that are written so true to life, readers will swear that they know some of them.

Minsky, Terri. *Lizzie McGuire, Vol. 1*. illus. TokyoPop. 2003. pap. $7.99. ISBN 1-59182-147-9.

Gr 4–5—Presented in cine-manga style, in which the illustrations are screen shots or cells used in the making of the television show, this book typifies Lizzie's life with all of its conflicts among her girlfriends and family members.

Runton, Andy. *Owly Volume 1: The Way Home & The Bittersweet Summer*. 2004. ISBN 1-89183-062-7.

——. *Owly Volume 2: Just a Little Blue*. 2005. ISBN 1-89183-064-3. ea vol: illus. by author. Top Shelf. 2004. pap. $10.

K Up—These two nearly wordless graphic novels tell of the adventures of an owl who just wants to make friends with those needing his help the most in the little woods where he makes his home.

SCIENCE FICTION

Kochalka, James. *Monkey vs. Robot*. 2000. $10. ISBN 1-89183-015-5.

——. *Monkey vs. Robot and the Crystal of Power*. 2003. $14.95. ISBN 1-89183-036-8. ea vol: illus. by author. Top Shelf. pap.
Gr 3–5—In these stories that exemplify a nature-versus-technology theme, a robot is out to ravage the habitat of a monkey, and an all-out war ensues between them. This is a great book for classroom discussions about the ecological effects of human intervention.

SUPERHEROES

Beatty, Scott. *JLA: The Ultimate Guide to the Justice League of America*. DK. 2002. Tr $19.99. ISBN 0-7894-8893-0.
Gr 4–6—Teachers and librarians will need this guide more than their students so they can catch up on all of the superheroes and their powers, rivals, and allies. Youngsters will love reading about the history of the characters as well as seeing the original art.

Buckley, James. *Creating the X-Men: How Comic Books Come to Life*. illus. DK. 2000. Tr $12.95. ISBN 0-7894-6694-5.
Gr 2–3—This easy-to-read chapter book employs the graphic novel format to explain the process of how X-Men comics are created, from initial concept through design to bookstore display.

Dini, Paul. *Wonder Woman: Spirit of Truth*. illus. by Alex Ross. DC Comics. 2001. pap. $20. ISBN 1-56389-861-6.
Gr 4–5—The beautiful artwork in this oversized graphic novel depicts the origins of this superheroine and how her quest for truth also promotes justice for evil crime doers.

Gallagher, John. *Buzzboy: Trouble in Paradise*. 2002. ISBN 0-972-18310-8.

——. *Buzzboy: Monsters, Dreams & Milkshakes*. 2003. ISBN 0-972-18311-6. ea vol: illus. Sky Dog Press. pap. $11.95.
Gr 4–5—These pop-culture-infused series entries feature a superhero-like character who enjoys milkshakes and too many hamburgers. Buzzboy is a crime fighter who would rather eat than fight.

Hibbert, Clare. *Wonder Woman's Book of Myths*. illus. DK. 2004. pap. $3.99. ISBN 0-7566-0242-4.
Gr 2–3—The Amazonian heroine shares her favorite stories of Greek gods and goddesses with young readers in this beginning chapter book.

Weigel, Jeff. *Atomic Ace: (He's Just My Dad)*. illus. by author. Albert Whitman. 2004. Tr $15.95. ISBN 0-8075-3216-9.
Gr 4–5—Told from the point of view of the middle school-aged son of a superhero, this story shows how the boy deals with his own emotions about his busy Dad, who misses

band concerts and other family events. But the boy realizes that his father's responsibilities of helping others can also be a source of pride.

ALLYSON A. W. LYGA *is a media specialist at Cranberry Station Elementary School in Westminster, MD, and coauthor of* Graphic Novels in Your Media Center: A Definitive Guide *(Libraries Unlimited, 2004).*

Graphic Novels in Today's Libraries[*]

By John Hogan
Graphic Novel Reporter, February 21, 2009

How are graphic novels viewed in libraries across the country today? While attitudes toward graphic novels and manga are changing, and librarians were among the first to change them, we wanted to learn more about how the formats are received and perceived today. So we asked some librarians to share their experiences. Their responses were fascinating.

We spoke with Eva Volin, head children's librarian in Alameda, California; Amy Alessio, teen coordinator for the Schaumburg Twp. Dist. Library in Illinois; David Serchay, youth services librarian for the Margate Branch of the Broward County Library System and author of *The Librarian's Guide to Graphic Novels for Children and Tweens* and *The Librarian's Guide to Graphic Novels for Adults*, and Arlene Allen, teen services librarian at the Main Library of the Broward County Library System. Here's what they had to say.

Tell us about the graphic novel sections in your library: Are they separated by age or interfiled with fiction and nonfiction? Please describe.

Eva Volin: We have three distinct graphic novels sections, one in children's, one in teens, and one in adult.

Amy Alessio: We have graphic novels in teen, adult, and youth collections. They are separated out under 741.5 in youth and adult and are separated out in their own large section.

David Serchay: In Broward County, graphic novels are cataloged in nonfiction, usually in the 741s (graphic nonfiction and biographies are cataloged in the appropriate number). They are also cataloged with age listings of juvenile (J), young adult (YA), and adult (no special prefix). Some libraries have their J, YA, and adult nonfiction sections separate from one another, while others have a combined nonfiction section. Some branches have also chosen to create a special graphic novel section in the library. Some of them are just J and YA, while others include adult-cataloged titles as well. In addition, what is owned by one branch can be sent to another if a patron requests it.

Arlene Allen: The Main Library does physically separate graphic novels by age—there are designated J, YA, and adult graphic novels.

Broward County offers an Interlibrary Loan service as well; graphic novels not in our holdings can be obtained from any library nationwide that participates in this service that carries the specific title.

Is funding for graphic novels separate, or is it part of the teen, adult, and youth collections?

Serchay: J and YA manga and graphic novels are a separate area of the overall Youth Services budget. Adult graphic novels are ordered from the adult fiction budget, but there is not separate "budget line" for them.

Alessio: Each age collection has funding for them. For example, teen GN funding is under teen collection, but its own budget line.

Volin: The funding for GNs is taken out of our general book fund. The book fund is broken out into children's, teen, and adult books.

Do you collect circulation statistics on the graphic novels? Do you know how they compare to the statistics for fiction and nonfiction titles?

Alessio: Yes. With a collection of 6,000, we circulate an average of 4,000 books a month. A little under half of those are graphic novels.

Volin: We don't pull statistics for specific sections. I can tell you that graphic novels tend to turn at least 2–3 times more often than general nonbestseller titles do.

Serchay: Generally they are just nonfiction stats, though that is often listed as YA nonfiction, and a large number of the YA nonfiction books are the graphic novels. If needed, we could get a listing of circulation for all titles in the 741s, but it is our understanding that when checked, circulation has been very high, and this is one reason that they have a separate budget and a graphic novel selection committee.

How much have the graphic novel and manga sections at your library changed over the past five years?

Volin: The children's GN collection is only 18 months old, and it has transformed and rejuvenated the children's section. Kids who had previously only used the library as a drop-in babysitting/computer service are now relaxing on the couches reading. Girls are devouring manga that is age-appropriate and mothers are discovering that comics actually improve reading skills. It's been a boon.

Serchay: They have greatly increased at a rate of over 1,000 titles a year (with an average of four copies per title). Many branches have also chosen to create a separate area for them.

Allen: In the case of manga, more than 500 volumes a year are published, so the library's collection in terms of both titles and volumes has grown significantly.

Alessio: Definitely GNs have grown at all three of our buildings. What we are seeing now is that with so many more publishers producing graphic novels, and different types of graphic novels, the old standby mangas and long-running series are not as popular. There is more to choose from.

How are graphic novels received by staff? By patrons? Is there a particular group who really seems to embrace them?

Alessio: The teens are certainly the most enthusiastic readers of GNs, but we do see many adults and younger children looking for them as well. At first, as with any new media, staff had to go through an education process. The cultural lines of acceptability were the hardest to teach. Now, though, it is an accepted and well-known collection in the library.

Volin: Some staff education was necessary—especially for those who understood the word *graphic* to mean "dirty." But seeing the books circulate as quickly as they do, and seeing the kids excited by the collection, and going on to pick up prose books when they are done with the comics, has converted most of the staff into believers.

Allen: Manga is primarily embraced by teens and young adults, although there are some adults often seen perusing the collection. Anime and manga clubs have an age range of about 11 through 23 years. Titles like *Naruto*, *Shaman King*, and other manga that have their companion anime series on television are also popular with children as young as 8.

Serchay: Most staff members appreciate that even if it's not something they like, the patrons do. Some branches have asked for more due to increased demand. As far as patrons go, all ages seem to enjoy them.

Who are the main patrons of graphic novels and manga in your library?

Volin: Primarily kids and teens. But we do have an impressive adult GN collection, so that area is building a diehard clientele, too.

Do you find it helpful when publishers put suggested ages on books? Do you follow those guidelines? What do you do when you are unsure which age group a graphic novel should be shelved under?

Volin: There are few things more useless than the "all ages" tag. Very few books will please an 8-year-old, a 20-year-old, *and* a 60-year-old. It's completely meaningless. Until the publishers standardize their ratings systems into something constant, the way the MPAA has done with movies, the less helpful the ratings on GNs will be.

Serchay: We do. YA tends to be the default designation if we are unaware of the proper area, and we adjust upward or downward when necessary.

Allen: We often visit comics shops and bookstores and read review publications to investigate certain titles further. Sometimes it is important to actually look at manga—especially that which is rated OT—because of cultural differences. What is accepted in terms of sexuality in Japan is regarded quite differently in America.

Alessio: We do find this helpful but are not limited by the suggested ages. When we are unsure, we consult with our local comic book dealer.

What special challenges are there in managing and maintaining the graphica section?

Alessio: Keeping the collection in order is hard with many huge series. It is not always possible to maintain the series alongside the standalones, due to space. So then finding the titles is somewhat challenging for staff at times, and many of the titles go missing or are beat up quickly.

Serchay: Theft is, of course, an issue, as is replacing titles. For example, when a volume of a manga series is missing, it needs to be replaced or else the story is incomplete.

Volin: Traditionally, fiction is alphabetized by author's last name or by Dewey number. With 14 different authors all writing *X-Men*, it can be very difficult for casual browsers to find what they're looking for. Libraries, if they want to be customer-friendly, need to adopt a bookstore model shelving system for their GN collections. Cataloging can also be a challenge, particularly with manga. Catalogers who are unfamiliar with GNs can be frustrated by how the entries should be formatted.

Do you feel the industry embraces graphic novels and why do you think so? In what way could more library staff learn about the genre? In what ways could library staff better promote graphic novels?

Volin: The library industry? Yes and no. I think the teen librarians have embraced GNs and are great about getting the books into libraries. But there are still so many libraries that are still getting started that we continue to need Beginning GN Collection–type workshops across the country. This isn't yesterday's news yet. For many library systems, this is still a new idea and we need to answer their questions with patience and respect.

Serchay: Libraries are embracing graphic novels because they realize that they are both popular and good. Library staff can learn more about the format (not a genre) by reading information online as well as the books on the subject. Graphic novels can be promoted by using such things as the Demco graphic novel stickers and standee and the posters by Demco and ALA. Programs for things like Free Comic Book Day can also be helpful, and also they include graphic novels in book displays either by themselves or mixed in with other books.

Allen: Classes and lectures on graphic novels and manga are helpful as well in helping staff members overcome preconceived notions and prejudices against the format.

Alessio: I think librarians were way ahead of the bookstore chains with the GNs. Many school media and public librarians were attending trainings and celebrating the genre years ago. After the Printz was given to *American Born Chinese*, I have noticed that having graphic novels is no longer a question for libraries. More library staff who are in locations where they do not have access to comic stores or conferences could utilize the YALSA Great Graphic Novels list or take online readers advisory courses for all ages, where they would find suggested graphic novels and traditional fiction as well.

We also offer writing and drawing classes by gentlemen who are published by DC and independent presses in those techniques. This has been a great way to further promote the collections.

Has the current economy affected your graphica collection yet? If so, how?

Serchay: Yes and no. While the overall youth services budget was lowered, the percentage that went for graphic novels has increased.

Allen: Of course, the graphic novel industry itself has been impacted. One manga company has cut its title production in half, and two others have gone out of business. Due to that, there may be fewer new manga titles on our shelves in 2009.

Volin: Only in that my materials budget is lower, so all of my buying is much more carefully done. If I'm buying fewer GNs, I'm also buying fewer everything else.

Alessio: Not yet. What we anticipate is a small collections budget, and more careful ordering.

Reinventing the Book Club[*]

Graphic Novels as Educational Heavyweights

By Jonathan Seyfried
Knowledge Quest, January/February 2008

We often find ourselves lamenting the loss of emergent readers to video games, television, and, most recently, the TTYL (talk/type to you later) culture of text messaging and Internet social networking. Trying to impart the joy of a good read to middle school students feels like pushing religion onto the perfectly content worshippers of American Idol. Yet, almost as if responding to a distress call, a new type of book has come onto the scene: the graphic novel. This revitalized genre has not only saved the day for recreational reading, it has also turned out to be a heavyweight in the teaching of advanced themes in literature and visual literacy.

When Brandeis Hillel Day School in San Francisco offered a library-sponsored book club as an elective class, no one ever imagined that we would have a waiting list. After one semester the Graphic Novels Book Group elective became the talk of the middle school. Further, students who had dutifully read only required books in the past, continued to return to the school library well after the elective was finished to check out prose fiction for recreational reading. The elective confirms the impact of a Graphic Novels Book Group on reading motivation.

It all began the previous year, when my colleague, head librarian Roz Tolson, and I were tossing around the idea for a librarian-led elective that could compete with attractive alternatives like Drama, Digital Video-Making, Triathalon, and Yearbook. With graphic novels sales estimated at over $300 million in 2006 (Publishers Weekly 2007) and the increased buzz in professional publications (Kan 2006), we decided to propose a Graphic Novels Book Group. After getting an enthusiastic reception from the Middle School administration, the stage was set for the Library's foray into the elective curriculum.

Before planning this elective, I could count on one hand the number of graphic novels I'd read. I considered the genre to be enjoyably quirky, but mostly irrelevant. As I sorted through the recommended lists and talked with the staff in a comic book store (collection development for graphic novels does not lend itself to ordering from reviews) and fellow librarians, I found myself struggling to select titles that would accommodate the wide variation in maturity I expected to find in our mixed sixth- through eighth-grade electives. I rejected *The Pride of Baghdad,* a story of the zoo animals who roamed the Iraqi streets during the chaos of the 2003 bombings. One full-page image of a giraffe's gruesome demise felt just too disturbing for our younger students. On the other hand, I did select *Persepolis,* which contains violent imagery, but depicted in a less violent, cartoonish style. By navigating this tricky line, I gained the respect of my students; they appreciated being trusted with mature content, and this led to greater investment in the class.

The graphic novel genre prides itself on its edginess. For example, the Action Philosophers comic book series by Fred Van Lente and Ryan Dunlavey is full of immature jokes, gratuitous violence, and crass imagery. It's also one of the best things published for philosophical education since the Symposiums. Students are introduced to complicated philosophical concepts without having to trudge through five hundred pages of academic prose. Our middle school students laugh at Karl Marx with an M-60, but they are only able to get the joke if they've understood concepts that most of us grappled to comprehend in college. The series was too edgy to be included as *required* reading for the elective, but we selected some for the library and they never stay on the shelf for more than half a day.

At the outset of the elective, there was quite a gap in experience among my students. Five didn't know what the term "graphic novel" meant, while the rest spent entire weekends sitting on the floor of the local bookstore devouring *manga.* Therefore I began with a discussion of the term "graphic novel" using the ideas outlined in Charles McGrath's watershed article in the July 11, 2004 issue of *The New York Times Magazine.* Graphic novelist Chester Brown drew the magazine's cover, a nine panel interview between a journalist and a graphic novelist. The graphic novelist in Brown's cover is defending himself against the accusation that his medium is "just comic books." He argues that "the scope for telling stories of greater complexity and depth is increased" (Brown 2004, cover) in longer comic books. When the story continues from the cover into the magazine (25), the interviewer has been transformed into a duck. Infuriated by this visual mockery, the novelist storms out of his graphic interview.

I ask the students why Chester Brown chose this little story to accompany an article that argues that graphic novels should be taken seriously, and that "comic books are what novels used to be" (McGrath 2004, 24). The students recognize at once that a comic book's tone is distinct from prose fiction. In Brown's comic, for example, the sequence from one panel to the next is tinged with both humor and irony. Unlike prose fiction, comics depict the passage of time visually, as the reader moves from one panel to the next. Artists such as Brown become masters at exploiting the kind of humor that arises from this type of narrative motion. In a snap, a human becomes a duck. Over the course of the semester, students continued to find other examples of this simultaneous use of both irreverence and a self-reflective silliness. And how twelve year-olds love self-reflective silliness!

What was remarkable to me, on that very first day of class, was that the students identified and responded to the poignancy of the stories immediately. The jokes, the conclusions, and the characters made sense at once. How often, I wondered, did they assimilate and understand assigned readings in their other classes so quickly? Throughout the elective I continued to be surprised by my students' responses. More than just an elective or a book group, our experience together went right to the heart of books and the joy of reading.

The structure of that first class determined how I approached each week's "lesson." For example, I continued to use readings, primarily from McCloud's *Understanding Comics* and its companion *Making Comics*, to apply to the graphic novels we read. McCloud's analysis of visual literacy is always accompanied by visual examples (the book itself is a long comic). He outlines a theory of comics as an art form and a mode of storytelling while modeling them in his drawings. We had animated discussions about the cultural and social implications of these texts. Different ideas appealed to different students. Some disputed whether McCloud's identification of ancient Mayan writing as proto-comics was accurate. Others focused on the role of visual storytelling in a visually saturated culture like ours, using examples of codes and signs based on McCloud's lucid explanation of semantics. Their engagement demonstrated to me what theorists like Janne Seppanen and McCloud postulate: that visual literacy is "the capacity to perceive the visible reality as part of broader cultural structures of meanings . . . the most essential thing thus is the understanding of the mechanisms of culture and the meaning of production in society" (Seppanen 2007, 133).

According to McCloud, every graphic novelist must make certain decisions when creating a page (or more) of panels. As we discussed each graphic novel we applied McCloud's "five choices" (2006, 37), a framework that helped students understand how a visual artist develops a meaningful image for a story. We discussed each decision—choice of moment, choice of frame, choice of image, choice of word, and choice of flow—to analyze what was being presented to the reader.

The sequential images on the final page of Guy Delisle's graphic novel travelogue, *Pyongyang* (see p. 44), can be analyzed with this framework. The page consists of three panels at the top, two in the middle, and three at the bottom. Delisle's *choice of moment* includes creating a paper airplane, a snapshot of the airplane mid-flight, and Guy Delisle, a character himself, watching and cheering from the window as the lonely paper airplane descends from the author's skyscraper hotel window. The first two panels show Delisle having the idea of making the airplane, and then beginning to fold it. The middle two panels show the flight of the airplane. The last three panels at the bottom of the page occur in an extremely close chronology, (perhaps not even seconds apart). In these almost identical panels, Delisle watches the plane cross the skyline.

In the middle two panels, *the choice of frame* (or context) juxtaposes the whimsical flight of a paper airplane against the stark Pyongyang skyline, emphasizing the emotional contrast in the story. The last three panels exclude most of the hotel room to focus the reader on the main character as he watches the plane out the window.

In one panel, for *choice of image,* Delisle draws the airplane on its own, separate from the person who threw it. This choice suggests the freedom that the paper airplane has from its creator, in contrast to the highly controlled lives of citizens in North Korea.

His *choice of words,* or rather lack of them, fits these themes. There are no words until the very last panel, reinforcing the understated tone of the whole novel. Finally, in the character's cheer "C'mon, go!" the reader becomes acutely aware of the poignancy of small rebellions in a repressive world.

For the *choice of flow,* or how the reader follows the sequence of the panels, Delisle imitates the journey of the airplane, with its curlicue trail sequentially on the last page. He could have concluded the book with a full page panel, or three panels in rows. Instead, his choice of three panels at the top, two in the middle, and three at the bottom creates a looping through the page as it is read. The flow of the story, through the panel arrangement, matches the flow of the airplane, the flowing of the curtains, and even the flow of Delisle's body hunched over the windowsill. In short, each choice on this magnificent last page contributed to evoking in the reader the emotions that accompany Delisle's futile resistance to North Korea's litter-free totalitarian regime.

Later that semester, another of our readings led to an exploration of themes in visual literacy—Gene Yang's National Book Award-nominated graphic novel, *American Born Chinese* (FirstSecond, 2006). In this graphic novel, the main character, Jin, is frustrated with being a cultural outsider in suburban America. He begins to see himself as his alter-ego, the blue-eyed, blond-haired, all-American boy "Danny." In turn, this Danny is haunted by a character that embodies all the stereotypes of Chinese people, a "cousin" named Chin-Kee. I introduced the students to a foundational theory in the symbolic interactionism school of sociology, Charles Horton Cooley's concept of "The Looking Glass Self," which suggests that we see ourselves as we imagine others see us ("Cooley, Charles Horton" 2005, 153–154). My students interpreted Yang's visual depiction of the characters and story as larger statements about the immigrant experience in America. One student said that *American Born Chinese* "showed exclusion and questioned what is 'normal.'" I was stunned that my students could learn to deeply question how cultures are shown and seen, an important aspect of visual literacy as Seppanen defines it:

> Visual literacy also means the ability to conceive the historical quality of visual orders and the power processes connected with them as well as to distinguish alternative orders. Visual literacy is thus not only an understanding of the visible reality, but at its best it is also the production of such presentations that challenge pictorial stereotypes connected, for instance, to the presentation of race and gender. (94)

In addition to being an excellent exercise in the understanding the presentation of race and ethnicity visually, *American Born Chinese* challenges readers' observation skills. The book consists of three separate and intertwining narratives involving Jin, Danny, Chin-Kee, and an archetype from Chinese mythology, the Monkey King. Deceptively simple at first reading, the structure builds a complex and extended metaphor and produces the poignant ending, which is easy to miss if read too fast. Therefore I encouraged students to read graphic novels slowly and, in fact, they often came to class having read the book twice. Successful readers of graphic novels learn that rereading and slow reading support close observation, a necessary skill of visual literacy.

For the last part of each class, the students worked on their own individual, forty-panel graphic novels. As creators and artists, they attempted to apply their understanding of the basic elements of visual storytelling. First, I asked them to develop a main character and a distinct beginning, middle, and end. Then we practiced learning to change scenarios (for example, "they're on a bad date") into storytelling ("my main character goes on horrible date after horrible date until she finds the right person"). Once they had created a character and plot, they turned to Comic Life (free software that comes with Mac OS) to create their visual stories. This easy-to-use software includes templates with pre-designed panel layouts and drag-and-drop speech bubbles. Creating their own comics consolidated what they were learning as readers. A few months after the class ended, one of my students said, "The class was different than a regular book group because we weren't just reading it, we were doing it too."

In my experience, middle school students are ready to engage with intense emotions, emotions that they are themselves experiencing for the first time, but they need appropriate material. My students crave stories that they can relate to, written in a language they can understand, with jokes they can get, and metaphors that are clear to them. What adults get from Jonathan Franzen, Dave Eggers, and Zadie Smith, my students got from Guy Delisle. Graphic novels provided them with a rich and rewarding literary experience at a time when the duration, vocabulary, and style of prose masterpieces cannot. A seventh grader marveled: "We didn't just read the story; we read the story behind the story."

This elective held surprises for everyone, including me. For example, I did not anticipate the ripple effects of this "reinvented" book club. At the beginning of the semester, some of my elective students felt that the library and the librarian had nothing to offer them for recreational reading. Now they regularly seek me out for fiction recommendations—and not just for graphic novels. One seventh-grade elective student has read both Mark Zuckas's *The Book Thief* and M. Anderson's *The Astonishing Life of Octavian Nothing*.

As my colleague, Roz Tolson, and I infuse graphic novels into other grades, we see similar leaps in reading. Fourth- and fifth-grade students, emboldened by their reading of long graphic novels like Jeff Smith's *Bone* and Larry Gonick's *Cartoon History of the Universe,* are now attempting sophisticated prose fiction. And our success is spreading. Our teaching colleagues have begun using graphic novels to increase students' confidence as readers and to develop their enjoyment of reading. Instead of heralding a regression from the art of the written word, we are finding that graphic novels are providing a new bridge to it.

TIPS FOR CHOOSING GRAPHIC NOVELS

- Read the whole graphic novel before adding it to the collection.
- Talk to people who already know about graphic novels, especially the managers at comic stores and librarians who have already done collection development in graphic novels.
- Read reviews, but don't purchase based solely on a review. Just one gory page could put a graphic novel over the line of what you are comfortable including in the school library. Be guided by selection criteria in your Selection Policy.
- Have a discussion with students about the responsibility that comes with reading mature content like *Persepolis* or *Action Philosophers*.
- Encourage younger students to read the more kid-friendly graphic novels, like Jeff Smith's *Bone* series.
- Watch out for the cheap low-quality graphic novels that lack discernible storylines. Trust your own instincts about quality and be picky.
- Limit the amount of manga (Japanese comic books) in the collection so that students will move beyond it to more sophisticated graphic novels and prose novels. Most series of manga can be given similar treatment in the library as prose series like *The Babysitters Club* or *Goosebumps*.
- There is not a single or standard age-rating system for graphic novels, so don't depend on the age ratings on the back covers. They are only general guides.

This article, a bibliography of graphic novels used in our book club, and sample of student work are available online: <www.ala.org/ala/aasl/aaslpubsandjournals/kqweb/kqarchives/volume36/363/363seyfried.cfm>.

JONATHAN SEYFRIED *is a librarian at Brandeis Hillel Day School. When not reading that latest graphic novel, he writes fiction and is currently working on a novel (not a graphic novel) for kids.*

WORKS CITED

Brown, Chester. "[Interview with a Graphic Novelist]." Comic strip. *New York Times Magazine* 11 July 2004: [cover].

"Cooley, Charles Horton." 2005. *Encyclopedia of Social Theory*. Vol. 1. Ed. George Ritzer. Thousand Oaks: Sage Publications. 153–54.

Kan, Kat. 2006. "Just what is it with graphic novels anyway?" *Knowledge Quest* 35, no. 1 (Sept.–Oct. 2006). <www.ala.org/ala/aasl/aaslpubsandjournals/kqweb/kqweb.cfm> (accessed Feb. 13, 2008).

McCloud, Scott. 1993. *Understanding Comics*. New York: HarperPerennial.

McCloud, Scott. 2006. *Making Comics*. New York: HarperPerennial.

McGrath, Charles. 2004. "Not Funnies." *New York Times Magazine* 11 July: 24+.

Publishers Weekly. 2007. "Graphic novels by the numbers." Editorial. 5 Mar.: 9. InfoTrac. Electronic. Thomson Gale.

Seppanen, Janne. 2006. "Power of the Gaze: an Introduction to Visual Literacy." *New Literacies and Digital Epistemologies* 20. N.p.: Peter Lang.

GRAPHIC NOVELS MENTIONED

Arakawa, Hiromu. *Full Metal Alchemist* (Viz, 2005).

Delisle, Guy. *Pyongyang* (Drawn & Quarterly, 2005).

Gaiman, Neil. *The Books of Magic* (DC Comics, 1993).

Gonick, Larry. *Cartoon History of the Universe* (Doubleday, 1990)

Hosler, Jay. *Clan Apis* (Active Synapse, 2000).

Kuper, Peter. *Franz Kafka's The Metamorphosis* (Crown, 2003).

Ottavani, Jim. *Dignifying Science* (G.T. Labs, 1999).

Satrapi, Marjane. *Persepolis* (Pantheon, 2003).

Smith, Jeff. *Bone* (Scholastic, 2005).

Stamaty, Mark. *Alia's Mission* (Random, 2004).

Telemagier, Rita. *The Babysitter's Club, Kristy's Great Idea* (Scholastic, 2006).

Vaughn, Brian. *Pride of Baghdad* (Vertigo, 2006).

Van Lente, Fred. *Action Philosophers* (Evil Twin, 2006).

Yang, Gene. *American Born Chinese* (FirstSecond, 2006).

Graphic Novels and School Libraries[*]

By Hollis Margaret Rudiger and Megan Schliesman
Knowledge Quest, November/December 2007

School libraries serving children and teenagers today should be committed to collecting graphic novels to the extent that their budgets allow. But the term "graphic novel" is enough to make some librarians—not to mention administrators and parents—pause.

"You're collecting *what* in the school library?"

UNDERSTANDING THE FORMAT

The first step in building a useful, appealing collection of graphic novels is to understand the format. Graphic novels are simply book-length comics. They can be works of fiction or nonfiction, and their content parallels the wide range of literature that librarians already collect in other forms, including biographies, poetry, and novels.

The term "graphic" in "graphic novel" means highly visual. It does *not* mean mature or violent content. Do some graphic novels have content, situations, and images that some might find upsetting or offensive? Absolutely, just as some novels have dialogue, violence, or sexual situations that may be upsetting; some picture books have images that may be distressing; and some nonfiction contains information that may be shocking.

The truth is that many if not all of the materials found on the shelves of school libraries have the potential to offend someone. As with any material in any library, it's important to look at the work as a whole and not take individual components out of context. And, as with any other kind of book—picture books, novels, nonfiction—graphic novels must be evaluated individually, not embraced or rejected as a whole.

IT'S ALL IN THE POLICY

While it is true that some people do have preconceived notions about, and even prejudices against, comics and graphic novels, it's important to maintain perspective. For school librarians, that means thinking about what graphic novels to collect in order to meet the needs and interests of the children and teens that the school library serves.

In other words, how do graphic novels fit into the collection development policy? It's a sure bet that graphic novels fit into existing policies in a number of ways. Remember, this is a format that embodies a wide range of material already being collected in school libraries, from biographies and other nonfiction, to adventure, fantasy, science fiction, contemporary realism, and historical fiction. As with other resources, they fulfill a variety of roles, from supporting the curriculum, to meeting students' need for leisure reading.

Some graphic novels will be purchased as "popular materials," others as books of information, and still others because of their literary merit. (These reasons are not necessarily mutually exclusive.) Whatever the reason, as long as collection development guidelines are followed, decisions can be made with confidence.

As with any publication, graphic novels vary widely in quality and content. Some are mediocre, and others are literary masterpieces. Just as you select any other item for purchase, turn to professional review journals or use whatever other criteria the library's collection development policy articulates to make selection decisions about graphic novels.

Here's welcome news: graphic novels now are commonly reviewed in professional library review journals. An increasing number of recommended graphic novel bibliographies have been developed for both school and public libraries. For a listing, visit the Cooperative Children's Book Centers (CCBC) Graphic Novels Resource page www.education.wisc.edu/ccbc/books/graphicnovels.asp

CATALOGING AND SHELVING

Now that you've decided to purchase graphic novels, the next step is deciding where to put them. Because graphic novels cover a wide range of subjects, some librarians choose to shelve titles by topic. For example, *Clan Apis* by Jay Hosler (Active Synapse, 2000) could be shelved in the science section, while *Persepolis: The Story of a Childhood* by Marjane Satrapi (Pantheon, 2003), could be placed with biographies.

Other librarians choose to catalog and shelve graphic novels based on their format, placing them all together. At the CCBC, for example, they are all shelved under 741.5, the Dewey number for comic books and graphic novels. While each method has merit, more librarians are choosing the latter. It creates a focal point for readers who might not be regular users of the library but are drawn in by graphic novel collections. While students cannot browse them by topic, the subject headings still enable readers to locate relevant titles to meet specific interests.

PROMOTION AND EDUCATION

If community members (including administrators, teachers, parents, students, and others) understand the benefits of graphic novels, they are less likely to challenge them due to misconceptions about the format or fears of the unknown. Consider holding a graphic novel discussion with students, staff, and parents. One useful question to pose is whether—and why—some people find visual images more problematic than words.

Look for opportunities to explain how graphic novels help the library meet its goal to support teaching and learning as well as the diverse needs and interests of the children and teens it serves. Create an attractive display that will allow individuals coming into the library to see the many kinds of storytelling and information to be found in the highly visual, or "graphic," format.

One librarian we know has a binder sitting beneath her display in which she has collected articles from many disciplines supporting graphic novels in education. Viewing the professional literature alongside the display, colleagues will begin to think about how they can capitalize on students' interest in graphic novels to further curricular goals related to visual literacy, media criticism, and nontextual information, as well as their potential for use with nontraditional learners, including students with some types of cognitive disabilities and those learning English. Ask for time during a staff in-service, or invite subject-area teachers to the library and map out how graphic novels may address their state standards in both content and skill areas. In short, be proactive in articulating the value of graphic novels to the school community.

And what if a complaint does arise, or a challenge does occur? Graphic novels are no different than any other resource in the library. Follow the procedures outlined in the school's collection development policy for informal and formal resolution of complaints about library materials—with confidence.

For additional ideas and information on collecting and using graphic novels in school libraries, we recommend Allyson and Barry Lyga's excellent *Graphic Novels in Your School Library Media Center: A Definitive Guide* (Libraries Unlimited, 2004) and the slightly older but still valuable *Graphic Novels 101: Selecting and Using Graphic Novels to Promote Literacy for Children and Young Adults: A Resource Guide for School Librarians and Educators* by Philip Charles Crawford (Hi Willow, 2003).

HOLLIS MARGARET RUDIGER *is formerly a Librarian with the Cooperative Children's Book Center of the School of Education at the University of Wisconsin—Madison. Her article "Graphic Novels 101: Reading Lessons" was published in* The Horn Book *in*

March 2006. She is currently serving on the 2008 YALSA/ALA Michael L. Printz Committee.

MEGAN SCHLIESMAN *is a Librarian at the Cooperative Children's Book Center of the School of Education at the University of Wisconsin—Madison. Megan manages the CCBC's Intellectual Freedom Information Services, including the library's online "What IF: Questions and Answers on Intellectual Freedom" forum. She currently serves on the board of the Wisconsin Library Association's Intellectual Freedom Roundtable.*

5

The People Behind the Pencils:
Conversations with Artists

Editor's Introduction

Not all graphic novels are created equal—nor are they created in the same way. The major comic book publishers, such as Marvel and DC Comics, own the rights to their characters and generally hire writers and artists to produce each work. These comics are almost always created by teams that also include inkers, letterers, and colorists. Other artists—such as the five profiled in this chapter—work more independently, overseeing their books from the sketching phase to the printing press.

In "A Comics Legend Draws on 9/11," this chapter's lead article, Dan DeLuca interviews Art Spiegelman, who won a Pulitzer Prize in 1992 for *Maus*. Whereas that book centers on the Holocaust, Spiegelman's *In the Shadow of No Towers*, released in 2004, tackles another heavy topic: the September 11, 2001 terrorist attacks on the World Trade Center and their aftermath. *No Towers* generated considerable political fallout upon publication, a subject Spiegelman does not shy away from in his conversation with DeLuca.

Lynda Barry started cartooning in the late 1970s, when she launched *Ernie Pook's Comeek*, a comic strip based on her childhood. In "Being Lynda Barry," Christopher Borelli interviews the writer and illustrator, who explains her decision to retire her renowned strip just shy of its 30th anniversary and talks about her other work in the graphic-novel field.

Robert L. Pincus profiles Daniel Clowes, who has written such comics as *Eightball* and *Ghost World*, in "'Scam' Artist," the subsequent entry in this section. In the piece, Clowes relates how he got started in the field and why he writes as well as illustrates his work. He also talks about comics of his that have been adapted into films.

In the following selection, "Life Drawing," Margot Harrison interviews Alison Bechdel, whose memoir *Fun Home* took the literary world by storm in 2006. Among the topics examined are Bechdel's work habits, her family life, why she wrote *Fun Home*, and how the book differs from her ongoing comic strip, "Dykes to Watch Out For."

For the next article, "Never Mind the Mullahs," Vivienne Walt spoke with Marjane Satrapi, author of the acclaimed *Persepolis*, a memoir about living in revolutionary Iran. Explaining to Walt why she chose to present the story in graphic-novel form, Satrapi downplays her skills as a traditional prose writer, insisting, "Images give me possibilities that I don't have with words."

In "Cartoon Politics," Michael Scott Leonard profiles comic artist Howard Cruse, whose work was featured in the Norman Rockwell Museum's 2007 "Lit-Graphic: The Art of the Graphic Novel" exhibition. Cruse recalls how becoming a cartoonist helped him accept his homosexuality while coming of age in Alabama.

Gene Luen Yang won the 2007 Michael L. Printz Award for his graphic novel *American Born Chinese*. In this chapter's final selection, Tom Spurgeon of *The Comics Reporter* talks with Yang about the impact of winning such a prestigious award and how it influenced his follow-up books. Spurgeon also asks Yang about specific aspects of his artwork—such as his page designs and penchant for single-color backgrounds—and the messages he wishes to convey.

A Comics Legend Draws on 9/11[*]

Pulitzer Winner Art Spiegelman Finally Follows Up His Holocaust Graphic Novel—with More Disturbing Visions

By Dan DeLuca
Philadelphia Inquirer, September 26, 2004

Art Spiegelman didn't know what to do for an encore.

It had taken 13 years, "long enough to be bar mitzvahed," to complete his groundbreaking, two-part graphic novel Maus—the harrowing tale of how his father, Vladek, survived the Holocaust. The book-length comic, which won the Pulitzer Prize, depicted Jews as mice and Germans as cats.

After its second part was published in 1992, "I felt like a farmer being paid not to grow wheat," Spiegelman says.

"One thing Maus did," says the 56-year-old cartoonist, "was scare the bejesus out of me as far as doing any more comics for a while. I would rather have gotten a lethal case of the flu than taken on another comic project after that."

That is, until Sept. 11, 2001.

The day the planes crashed into the World Trade Center towers—at the foot of which Spiegelman's daughter, Nadja, had begun high school three days earlier—the cartoonist vowed to get back to making comics.

The terror attacks on his lower Manhattan neighborhood jolted him into creating the 10 dazzling color plates collected in his new book, In the Shadow of No Towers (Pantheon, $19.95), one neurotic New Yorker's frantic, self-involved political broadside created in reaction to "a global tragic event that was one of those hinge moments, when the way the world is aligned changed."

The oversized volume, published on heavy cardboard like a children's book, opens to reveal inventive strips whose tumbling, vertical structures evoke the massive scale of the towers themselves. A computer-generated image of the skeleton of the second tower, "glowing, awesome as it collapses," haunts the pages like an inescapable nightmare.

"I tend to be easily unhinged," Spiegelman writes in the introduction. "Minor mishaps—a clogged drain, running late for an appointment—send me into a sky-is-falling-tizzy. It's a trait that can leave one ill equipped for coping when the sky actually falls."

And yet, "disaster is my muse," writes Spiegelman, who often draws himself as a mouse.

"There aren't that many pages, and each one is more like a painter's plate, or a portfolio, than a narrative comic, or a graphic novel, as they've come to be called," says Spiegelman, who's worn an upside-down peace sign pinned to his vest since Sept. 11. He chain-smokes Camels as he talks in his spacious studio ("the house that Maus built") on the first morning of Rosh Hashana, the Jewish New Year. "And then there are all these old comics at the back, which I think of as the book's second tower."

Those old comics are early 20th-century newspaper strips such as Windsor Mc-Kay's spectacular Little Nemo in Slumberland and Lyonel Feininger's The Kin-der-Kids Abroad. Like No Towers, they were oversized comics produced in a turbulent, politically fractious era.

"They brought me back to lower Manhattan near ground zero in 1901, where newspaper comics were first invented," he says. "After those towers that were built to last fell down, ephemeral things like newspaper comics began to seem more tangible."

Believing that the Bush administration "hijacked" the tragedy and turned it into a "war recruitment poster," Spiegelman portrays himself in the book as "equally terrorized" by al-Qaeda and the U.S. government. Conked out at his drawing table, he's flanked by Osama bin Laden, who holds a bloody saber, and George W. Bush, with a pistol and American flag.

Spiegelman completed the first of the No Towers pages in the summer of 2002, but in the runup to the war in Iraq, the cartoon's antigovernment slant found no takers in the mainstream American press. (The strip's only U.S. publisher was the Jewish weekly newspaper the Forward.)

"I'd gotten spoiled over the decades, because my work was in demand," says Spiegelman. He has contributed to the New Yorker, where his wife, Francoise Mouly, is art editor, including a 1993 Valentine's Day cover depicting a Hasidic Jewish man kissing an African American woman. He and Mouly edited Little Lit, two volumes targeted at preteens, and he published The Wild Party, illustrations accompanying Joseph Moncure March's ribald Jazz Age poem.

Spiegelman also drew the famous black-on-black cover image of the World Trade Center for the first post-Sept. 11 issue of the New Yorker. But the magazine wasn't interested in No Towers.

"It has to do with the scrim through which the New Yorker sees the world. It assumes an intelligence but also a bemused detachment. . . . The tone isn't one of engagement. It's hard to shriek out, 'The sky is falling! The sky is falling!' because your monocle will fall off."

Spiegelman found his "coalition of the willing" among newspaper publishers in Europe, where, he jokes, he was regarded as "a skinnier and less on-message Michael Moore."

Though it has drawn some positive reviews, No Towers has also raised hackles. In one panel of the book, a poster reads, "MISSING: A. Spiegelman's Brain, last seen in lower Manhattan, mid September 2001." A Time magazine reviewer suggested that No Towers offered little evidence it has yet been found.

When the Republican National Convention came to town last month, Spiegelman wore a "pray for a secular future" shirt and protested along with his wife, 17-year-old daughter and 12-year-old son, Dashiell. The author of Maus is not an observant Jew—"but I observe Jews," he cracked.

"I'm a total diasporist. I like the outsider, skeptical, questioning Jewish tradition that ultimately includes Marx, Freud and Kafka." After he skipped out of synagogue on Yom Kippur at 14 to eat a slice of sausage pizza and didn't get struck by lightning, he figured "all bets are off."

Spiegelman recently completed a libretto for Drawn to Death: A Three Panel Opera, a collaboration with musician Phillip Johnston of the Microscopic Quintet, which tells the history of comics in the 20th century.

He's also at work on a new comics project: "Some of it is historical, some of it is fiction, some of it is autobiography," he says. "Doing No Towers, this narcissistic take on a cataclysm much larger than me, let me develop this sort of fractured storytelling style that I'm interested in trying out on other things."

Spiegelman's importance to the world of comics for grownups reaches beyond Maus, which is widely acknowledged as the high-water mark of the medium that, Spiegelman jokes, is often still regarded as "the twisted hunchback dwarf of the arts."

In the 1980s and early 1990s, Spiegelman and Mouly edited Raw, an influential journal that gathered work of such young artists as Gary Panter, Ben Katchor and Philadelphia's Charles Burns, and Spiegelman is a tireless advocate for the work of rising cartoonists such as Chris Ware and Daniel Clowes. He has no plans to revive Raw, however.

"I don't think it's needed now," Spiegelman says. "There's more good work being produced right now than any time I can remember. As the world is turning to s---, it seems to be a great time for comics."

Being Lynda Barry[*]

For The Legendary Cartoonist, It's Been a (Very Bumpy) Road Less Taken

By Christopher Borrelli
Chicago Tribune, March 8, 2009

"There's a gas leak."

That's the first thing Lynda Barry said to me. Then she looked at me sideways, like a shy child, and though it was late summer and uncommonly pleasant, conducive to an outdoors interview, she led me into the living room, where we talked for hours, enveloped by disorienting fumes, which grew in pungency by the minute. She wore a red bandanna, which she wears a lot; a white shirt because she sweats a lot; glasses with lenses so thick they reminded me of an aquarium; and intense red lipstick, because that's her uniform. "The great thing about leaving Chicago for Wisconsin," she said, "is Wisconsin's full of eccentrics." "There's no pressure to be straight. You might think there is. But they know I'm a nut. There are a lot of nuts here, which is good because the thing I can't do is tamp down the way I look. This is as straight as I get. I look crazy. I know I do. Been true since I was a kid! I looked like Alfred E. Newman. Now look at me!"

Not much has changed—not since the last time we saw Lynda Barry. If you first read her in the 1980s, or got to know her during one of her appearances on "Late Night with David Letterman," it's all still there. Her sweaty awkwardness remains, as does her effusive warmth. And yet everything has changed. If you've heard of her, you remember "Ernie Pook's Comeek," her stinging comic strip about her (thinly veiled) childhood. Or you recall "The Good Times Are Killing Me," her Off-Broadway play about a racially mixed neighborhood, which started in Chicago. Or you read "Cruddy," her violent road-trip novel that became a staple of hipster bookshelves. In which case, her art still bears the mark of a distracted doodler, and her writing, simultaneously bitter and open-hearted, remains the voice of a wounded child, with the bittersweet notes of an adult who has not forgotten a thing.

That said, in October, so quietly even her close friends didn't know, the 52-year-old stopped drawing "Ernie Pook's Comeek." She stopped shy of the comic's 30th anniversary, which should have been this year. The strip began in the Chicago Reader, where it had taken on the feel of wallpaper, always there.

When I asked her why she quit, she said she was syndicated in only four papers anyway. A decade ago, she was in 70 alternative weeklies. Meanwhile, the Reader was paying $80 a week, the same as in 1979, and other papers were paying $25 a week—in other words, she was getting $155 a week for the strip that made her reputation, landed her on Letterman, got her a deal with HarperCollins, launched a brilliantly stubborn career, and became an inspiration to a generation of cartoonists with memoirs in their heads. She did not seem [fazed], though. In moments like this, Barry strikes a casual voice. She says, "It felt like an ax to the forehead." Then, after a moment, "It's cool."

It's cool because, even as she is waning as a weekly presence, she has a gathering sainthood within the comics community, a sense of impending canonization alongside cartooning legends like R. Crumb.

Consider this from cartoonist Chris Ware, one of her strongest supporters: "I say with absolute conviction that, just as Charles Schultz created the first sympathetic cartoon character in Charlie Brown, Lynda was the first cartoonist to write fiction from the inside out—she trusted herself to close her eyes and dive down within herself and see what she came up with. We'd still be trying to find ways into stories with pictures if she hadn't."

If one way of measuring an artist's importance is output, then Barry is nearing a new peak—next month brings the release of her next book, "The Nearsighted Monkey," and a year from now, a 10-volume reprint of every Lynda Barry strip ever. Asked about her slow resurrection, Matt Groening, the creator of "The Simpsons" and Barry's best friend, says simply: "I do see it beginning to happen—and it's overdue."

Cartoonist Ivan Brunetti, who grew up on the South Side reading Barry and teaches art at Columbia College Chicago, wastes no words: "She's become one of the most important cartoonists we have—however quietly people are recognizing it. She was first to do fictional comics that felt autobiographical, which is the draw today with graphic novels, and she was the first strong female voice in comics. But most importantly, I think it's become increasingly known that she moved the medium closer to real literature."

The first time they met, Brunetti says, Barry had asked a handful of friends back to her hotel room for drinks. "While we were all sitting there, she asked if anyone had ever thought seriously about killing someone and how they would do it. It was hilarious and random, and you know, as left-field as it sounded, these people had shrewd, detailed plans. But then she knew they would."

The day of the gas leak, Barry and I were sitting in the living room of Kelly Hogan, the Chicago torch singer, who splits her time working as Barry's assistant and recording with singer Neko Case. Hogan moved here, eight miles from Barry's farm (which is an hour from Madison), in May, in part to be closer to Barry.

Barry moved to Wisconsin with her husband in 2002, after being priced out of Evanston. Thus began, more or less, a self-imposed isolation. She rarely saw friends, sometimes not leaving the house for weeks. Asked why, she sounded earnest and evasive: "Something disconnected around 2000, some wire came out of the wall."

Meanwhile, the gas was enveloping us, stinging like chlorine. There was a black poodle with watery eyes curled at her feet, and as I listened to her, I began to wonder if I would die. Walls tilted. My vision blurred.

I heard Barry explain that the dog at her feet was named Ed Martin, but he appears in her comics under the pen name of Fred Milton, and that she has a lot of dogs, and that Ooola, the shepherd mix she found in a shelter and wrote about in "One! Hundred! Demons!," her 2002 "autobiofictionography," had died, and I said all of the dogs in her comics tend to look like this dog, and she said, "Turns out with dogs, you can pretty much have the same dog over and over, looks-wise."

Hogan poked her head in.

"Going to Piggly Wiggly," she said.

"Have fun," Barry said.

"Anything?"

"At the Pig, no."

"Back soon. Need to fry up some okra before the guy shows up to shut off that gas."

The wooden front door slammed against the wooden frame. Barry looked at me and grinned.

A few weeks later on a bright fall morning, I was back in Wisconsin, headed for Barry's farm, when I found myself behind an old pickup, whose bumper sticker read, in letters that suggested overinflated tomatoes, "Oh, What a Friend We Have in Cheeses." A dog ran alongside my car for what seemed a mile, then dropped and scratched at its stomach. The truck was so slow, my mind started to wander. I had recently taken Barry's writing workshop, one of her few sources of income now. The central exercise, which she learned from her beloved college art teacher Marilyn Frasca, was to visualize and catalog an image in your head. I did this to pass the time, focusing instead on my surroundings: fields sprawling into the distance, coming to rest at far-off strip malls; above, a cloud in the shape of Connecticut. Behind, pavement, silos, an occasional cow.

These days, Barry generally wants to talk about two things—the wind farm industry, which she spends most of her time opposing; and this writing workshop, a two-day seminar called "Writing the Unthinkable," which is meant to remove the angst from creativity. Hogan books it around the country and Barry gives her half the profits.

So popular is the course, it recently spawned a book, "What It Is," which itself is so unusual that the word "book" seems wrong. Picture yellow notebook paper crammed with watercolors of octopi and drawings of Snoopy and text loaded with memories of growing up without encouragement and collages of clipped magazine photos and doodles of the Virgin Mary. The point is delivering advice on how to free your inner writer. It's hard to believe it was published at all, never mind that Montreal-based Drawn & Quarterly has gone through three printings (and sold 30,000 copies).

To flip through it is to feel adrift in someone's daydream. "What I teach with the book and the course," she tells me, "is a physical activity, which is doodling when you're not writing, which itself should induce a state of mind. Which is getting yourself to the place you are when someone tells a joke. You're open, right? It's the place you go when your body's asleep and you can feel the dream starting to come on. I try and get calm so the ideas don't go away. I let it come slowly. Then as the ideas come I write slower. Which may sound counterintuitive! But you don't have to catch ideas. They're like the ocean around you."

Thus Barry's work, she says, is never premeditated. She never considers what to draw or write until she begins. ("Ernie Pook," and its menagerie of sticky child characters, never had anything like a plot.)

When she shows me the novel she's finishing, about a man who decides he's not going to live long enough to write a book so he creates the spines of books he might have written, she reveals how she's been writing it, i.e. she paints each sentence, each letter, in watercolors—so slowly, you wonder how she recalls what she's writing about.

Barry lives on a long county road without a name, just a letter. After a few minutes of manicured fields, I spot her farm—a modest 12 acres, a short jog from the town of Footville (pop. 770). Kelly Hogan had said I couldn't miss it, "the most plant-happy, overgrown-looking farm on that road—very natural, yellow aluminum siding, pole barn, white buildings, tin rooftops, dogs barking their asses off." No joke: Barry's farm is a Munsters homestead at the edge of a Mayberry town, but in a nice way. Designed by her husband, Kevin Kawula—who, for six years, has relentlessly pruned its non-native plants while reintroducing more natives— its grasses grow high and undulate in the wind. Sunflowers tower. Bluebirds dart. Four times a day Barry walks the quarter-mile path carved into the curled grass. We trudge. She breathes lightly. She leads me to a grain silo and pokes her head in, twists her body to look up, shouts into the empty tower, pulls her head out, and says, "Love doing that."

Her home is smaller than her barn, which contains a grizzly bear's head, a vintage pickup, and, dangling from a beam, a Cuddly Dudley puppet, a souvenir of the old WGN kiddie show "Ray Rayner and His Friends." She stumbled on it at the local Dig n' Save. The centerpiece of the farm, though, is her studio. It took Kawula more than a year to build it. The windows are wide and wrap around, so the studio resembles a wooden spaceship at the heart of a vast field. She can watch storms approach from here. Every cranny is packed, with paperbacks, DVDs, CDs, a furnace, a bathtub without feet, a bathroom, a painting by Chris Ware, an elaborate model home (from an auction), stuffed dolls losing stuffing, cigar boxes, dioramas, toppling piles of National Geographic and, in a corner, her work table.

She opens a drawer. Paper explodes like a can of coiled snakes. "This pile here," she says, lifting up a stack of disorganized paper, "this will become my next novel."

I grab a phone book from a pile of phone books—she hates wasting paper and so every page, every surface, is covered with paintings and letters, each precisely the same height. But it's idyllic.

You can see why someone would hole up here—and why she is scared a proposed wind farm may be built less than a mile away. When she's not working on her comics, she's organizing against the wind industry, building Web sites, attending meetings, arguing against the environmental (and aesthetic) cost. "There will be no horizon anymore," she fumes. "People forget about motion sickness. The flicker from the shadows they throw!" She said she feels like part of the French Resistance—she's the cartoonist, thrown together with an assortment of locals, most more conservative than she's used to socializing with.

They ask what kind of books she writes. She tells them "horror"—which isn't far from the truth.

She was born in Wisconsin, moved to Seattle with her Filipino mother at age 4. Her father, a butcher, left when she was young. The gory details are in her strips—the mother a cartoon gargoyle, the trailer parks where she lived, the casual cruelty of friends and family.

"It was Bizarro World. Everything backward. My mom didn't want me to go to college. She didn't want me to read—when I read, I may as well have been holding a pineapple." Barry lived a block from school and would arrive before dawn. The janitor would let her in. She would help take down chairs. She gravitated to the teachers. When school closed for the night, she would hang around until the last teacher drove away from the parking lot.

Alison Bechdel, who had great success a couple of years ago with "Fun Home," a graphic-novel memoir about growing up with a troubled father, said she remembers, as a teenager, reading Barry every week and thinking, " 'Good God, what kind of childhood did this person have?' It's remarkable for someone to do a brilliant piece now and then. But for 30 years, with that level of consistency? That's a staggering accomplishment. What's frightening is how much access she has to her subconscious."

I ask Barry why she has never moved beyond childhood, and she says, "I don't know. I don't know. I think maybe because those years are vivid. We don't have money at that age, so we can't buy our way out of a situation. We can't drive away. You're on foot a lot. You see a lot on foot."

I ask if she liked "Peanuts." She says she appreciates it now, but hated it at the time—too melancholy for a sad child. She liked "Family Circus"—"You know how everything's in a circle? I wanted to reach into it." She recently met Jeff Keane, the son of "Family Circus" creator Bil Keane. She says she touched his hand and burst into tears.

Matt Groening says he tried to get Barry to go Hollywood in the '80s. "I said to Lynda, 'Let's write a romantic comedy,' and she agreed." A pitch meeting followed at a Los Angeles movie studio. Groening remembers walking into the executive's enormous office, where Barry immediately moved toward a cagelike sculpture in the corner and stood inside it.

"That was the high point," Groening says. When they sat on the sofa, Barry cheerfully told the exec that it was Groening's birthday.

"Happy birthday," the exec replied.

"It's not," Groening said.

"It is," Barry said.

"It's not," Groening said.

"Lynda insisted it was," Groening remembers. "I gave up and said 'Yes, it's my birthday.' I looked crazy."

Afterward, Groening was mortified. Barry remembers spittle plastering Groening's windshield. She says he was frothing at the mouth. Groening remembers his car shaking, but doesn't recall the spittle.

In any case, according to Barry, Groening felt she was torpedoing her career. He felt she wasn't taking herself seriously enough.

But even now, Groening describes Barry as his oldest and dearest friend. They met at Evergreen State College in Olympia, Wash., in the early 1970s. Groening says it was the kind of school where the word "class" was forbidden, but "group contract" was OK. There were no grades. He was the editor of the school newspaper and heard about a girl in a nearby dorm who wrote to Joseph Heller, author of "Catch 22." She had asked Heller to marry her and Heller had written back to politely decline, citing his unwillingness to live in a dormitory.

Groening and Barry became friends, and when he began writing for the Los Angeles Reader, an alternative weekly, Groening would tell everyone about Barry. Bob Roth, at the Chicago Reader, read her stuff and remembers hiring Barry because it "made telling observations about real life, which is also what the Reader aspired to at the time."

According to Barry, the sale of a single comic to Roth paid the rent.

Steadily, though slowly, her strip caught on and became a standard of alternative weeklies across the country. Groening remembers her being successful enough to talk about buying real estate.

He also remembers once proposing to Barry, though they were just friends: "I was visiting her in Seattle and she says I was drunk but I wasn't. I was a typical bachelor standing in an apartment saying, 'You know, we could get married.' Her response was 'The hell!'"

By the late '80s–early '90s, at the peak of her success, Barry was a force of nature, says Heather McAdams, whose own deeply personal, untitled comics became ubiquitous for a short time—part of a handmade, ratty-at-the-edges Chicago scene of zines, roots rock and neighborhoods not yet gone condo. McAdams says that before Barry moved to Chicago in 1989 (bringing along her then-boyfriend Ira Glass), they were pen pals. When they met for the first time, "she came charging into the room and jumped on top of me and was yelling, 'Look at you! You have a bigger smile than I do! You're beautiful!'"

As McAdams tells it, she and Barry would climb on stage at (the long defunct) Lounge Axe and sing Loretta Lynn songs. Barry would stick her fist into her mouth. They wore cowboy boots and red lipstick and were loud. Sometimes they hung out at Fitzgerald's. For years the pendulum on the Berwyn club's grandfather clock had a photo stuck to it of Barry dancing. They lived around the corner from each other and talked every day.

By the mid '90s, however, Barry had met Kawula, a prairie restoration expert. "Chicago was like a big party for a while," Barry said. "It was fun, but you don't want to live at the party."

She and McAdams stopped speaking (they're vague on why). Barry married Kawula and stopped using the phone—with editors, with everyone. Editing, press interviews—it was all by fax.

Barry was writing. Her novel, "Cruddy," was a success, but the publisher, Simon & Schuster, did not solicit any new work. At HarperCollins, which published some of her early cartoon collections, her editor left. Harper did not request new comics.

With her career threatening to become anorexic, Barry moved to Wisconsin. Slowly, compilations of her comics slid out of print. At the same time, alternative newspapers began to fold and consolidate. She had some modest success with Portland, Ore.-based Sasquatch Books—but that relationship fell apart too. So she began to sell work on eBay (her best source of cash these days). But primarily, she began to panic.

Then Chris Ware stepped in. Ware, whose graphic novel "Jimmy Corrigan: The Smartest Kid on Earth" made him one of the top contemporary cartoonists, had met Barry when he was in his 20s. She sent him "lengthy and inspiring letters," he says, "which kept me alive artistically when my self-confidence was at its lowest, an act of supreme generosity—I barely have time to answer the phone now let alone write six-page letters of encouragement to young cartoonists."

Last year, Ware found his chance to repay her: Chris Oliveros, the publisher of Drawn & Quarterly, the most adventurous publisher of graphic novels, had been anxious to work with Barry. But he couldn't reach her and assumed she was already contracted with another publisher. Ware connected them. And so, this spring, D&Q will release "The Nearsighted Monkey," followed by the 10-volume reissue of Barry's comic strip work.

"It felt like Katrina," Barry says. "The water's building. Then Chris Ware shouts, 'Hey, there's a cartoonist in that attic!' "

Francoise Mouly, art director of the New Yorker, says she had been sad about Barry for a long time "because I wasn't sure she was even doing comics anymore, not in any serious way. The last time I saw her in New York [last fall], she looked invigorated. I couldn't help think 'Lynda's back from the dead.' We should all have a self-imposed isolation in Wisconsin."

I asked Groening if he felt guilty about the disparity in their careers, and Groening says he's learned to back off. Barry has had a number of solid offers to adapt her strips to animation, but she and Groening have irrevocably different approaches.

Says Groening, "I work with a huge number of people and I do this thing that's mainstream and pop culture and she's extremely personal. She is a master of the handwritten gesture. What I do is invariably collaborative. She transforms the ordinary into extraordinary, moving art but she is sensitive and I wouldn't want her to deal with the personalties."

Barry agrees—she doesn't collaborate well. As Groening puts it, when he looks at Barry, he does see the road less traveled. "We have a parallel universe thing going," he says. He could never live in Wisconsin, and she hates Los Angeles. He hates that she sells her art on eBay, and she says it's the only way a cartoonist as independent as she is can eke out a living.

Says Barry, "Matt is the kind of guy who likes to get telemarketers so he can screw with them." And Barry, says Groening, has embraced the idea of the teacher who changes lives. Indeed, when I took her two-day course, she ended by looking each student in the eye then screaming an effusive "GOOD! GOOD!"

The difference between their paths, as well as their fortunes, is stark. In the 1980s, when they were known as the king and queen of underground comics, Barry and Groening would do joint book signings. But Groening would always have a huge line and Barry would sit patiently waiting for anyone. A customer once asked her where the history section was.

Likewise, at the New Yorker Festival last October, one of the hottest tickets was an interview with Barry, conducted onstage by Groening. Tickets sold out in minutes. But Groening was the attraction—so much so that Barry worried that the audience would be disappointed with it being all Barry, and she insisted that a clip of "The Simpsons" be shown. When the two of them took questions, nearly all went to Groening. Barry listened, eyes twisted in concentration, nearly motionless; it's a talent she's had since childhood, she says, a near-supernatural ability to remain still for a long time.

Then a woman stood, sounding near tears. She told Barry that she grew up in Chicago and waited each week for a new "Ernie Pook." She said, "I want you to know how thankful I am for your creative choices. It's just a comic but it was important to me." Barry had a blubbery smile of profound gratitude. I'd seen that look before, a month earlier at a bar 10 miles from her home. We were eating cheeseburgers and she told me a story about Kelly Hogan. She said Hogan was leaving Neko Case's tour bus one night when she stepped on a cream doughnut.

"She slid on it, across the parking lot, really hurt her foot. One of the band members left the tour bus to have a look at the trail of cream and then he went back into the tour bus and looked at Kelly and said, 'Well, at least you rode it a while.' And that's exactly how I feel at the end of the day. This whole cartoonist thing—at least I rode it a while."

'Scam' Artist*

Daniel Clowes Tapped Into the Absurdity of Formal Schooling for Comic Books, Films and a Career

By Robert L. Pincus
San Diego Union-Tribune, July 16, 2006

Daniel Clowes, a major contemporary comic book artist and holder of a BFA in art, once called art school "the biggest scam of the century." He wrote these words in the early 1990s, but it's hard to think he's changed his mind.

Becoming disillusioned with what art school turned out to be was a marvelously fortunate twist of taste for Clowes. It gave him a storyline in one of his early comics (in 1991, to be exact) that ultimately became his second feature film, "Art School Confidential," released a few months ago. (The line about the scam is from the original comic strip.)

His first film, the critically lauded "Ghost World," which came out in 2001, also used an art class to sardonically comic effect, even if that wasn't part of the graphic novel. The screenplay for "Ghost World," co-written by Terry Zwigoff, the film's director, and Clowes, earned them an Academy Award nomination.

Don't read him wrong. Clowes, mostly self-taught, admires great art. It's just poseurs, like the hilariously pathetic Professor Sandiford or the loud-mouthed, loopy and self-important film student Vince in "Art Confidential," that end up getting skewered.

Clowes, now 45, is one of the most visible figures in the rise of the graphic novel. "Ghost World" has sold more than 100,000 copies, which, according to his long-time publisher's Web site, is "the bestselling book in Fantagraphics' 29-year history not involving beagles."

He's been coming to Comic-Con since the early 1990s, when he was the obscure creator of the first installments in his "Eightball" series (now numbering 23 issues). This year, he's a showcased speaker (on Thursday at 4:30 p.m.) and part of a Fantagraphics panel on Friday. He'll be signing books, too, over the course of his three-day visit (ending Saturday).

In spite of his art school training and his recent success with movies, Clowes remains passionate about his core activity.

"Comics are their own world," he says, talking by phone from the home in Oakland he shares with his wife Erika and son Charlie. "I'll continue to do comics because I really like the idea of comic books, even though the publishing world isn't set up for them."

His comics career began when his attempt to become a magazine illustrator failed. He spent a year in New York trying to get work, after graduating from Pratt Institute in Brooklyn. There wasn't enough work, and what there was turned out to be dull. So, he returned to his hometown, Chicago.

In 1985, he debuted "Lloyd Llewellyn," and began developing the stripped-down visual style, in its seven issues, that he would refine in the "Eightball" series that followed. ("Art School Confidential" was in "Eightball #7" and "Ghost World" unfolded in several installments.)

He culled from a host of sources to develop his own stark look, including vintage EC comic book artists like Johnny Craig and Bernie Krigstein, Mad magazine, old horror films (mostly of the B variety), film noir and pop art. His original style is evident even in an early series, assembled as the graphic novel with the vivid title "Like a Velvet Glove Cast in Iron." It makes masterful use of black and white in a story that is science fiction turned surreal.

Black and white was a necessity for economic reasons, but Clowes set out to make a virtue of the situation.

"I thought: I want to push the uses of black and white," he says. "I want 'Velvet Glove' to have the feel of a 3-in-the-morning black-and-white film with Robert Culp. I still remember the thrill of watching black-and-white TV when you're 8 years old."

Still, the sex, violence and psychological tensions push "Velvet Glove" beyond that Culp criteria, though looking at its pictorial style and clipped dialogue makes his analogy useful. The close-ups on faces, the select distortions of figures and striking uses of blacks and grays make the book as much visual as narrative. And Clowes' style fits the unsettling, dark nature of the story.

"Writing that story, I was tapping into weird dreams that I couldn't get out of my head," he confides. "They were arresting images from my conscious and unconscious mind and I didn't edit them."

Though renown has brought Clowes more chances to exhibit his work in galleries, he doesn't see the wall as the ideal environment for his drawings.

"They're drawn specifically with the eye and the lap in mind. That is, the art is done with the comic book or book in mind."

The challenge, as he defines it, is not to tilt the story too much toward writing or visuals.

"When I'm reading really well-written novels, I find that my descriptions get wordy. When you're writing for comics, you need a sense of how they each work.

My goal is for the reader to be unaware of themselves looking at individual panels as they experience the story."

He's never liked the term "graphic novel." Clowes has fought it for years, but he admits that he's lost this battle.

"Cartooning is accurate to some degree," he says. "I like to think of what I do as just a comic book. That sets the expectations as low as possible. But now even my elderly relatives know about graphic novels. It's a useful term now, but inaccurate."

By default, then, he's become one of its main practitioners. And by default, he's become a writer. He's ambitious on both counts, expanding the definition of the graphic novel like his friend Chris Ware.

Drawing was always Clowes' forte. When he decided, after Pratt, that he wanted to create comics, Clowes thought he would "team up with a writer."

Fortunately, he never quite found the right person.

"In school, I was a good enough writer to get by, though I didn't take great pleasure in it. And as a child, I was sort of a storyteller. I would make up weird stories that weren't entirely true.

"Writing for comics, you need a sense of how they work," he adds. "Now, I sometimes think I have more of a knack for writing than drawing."

"Ghost World" and "Art School Confidential" demonstrate his flair for film writing too. These coming-of-age stories expand on the comic book versions: the first a tale of Rebecca and Enid, whose friendship carries them though crises of sex, work and amusing encounters with eccentrics; the second an account of Jerome Platz's struggle to become an artist without sliding into utter cynicism about what he discovers about art school and the art world.

Clowes teamed again with Zwigoff as director on "Art School Confidential," but many critics were cool to their second collaboration.

"Art critics and older artists loved it," Clowes observes. "Movie critics as a group didn't like it. I want to look at that and analyze it a bit. But I'm happy with what I wrote and I can't second-guess it."

His entry into the film world was "pure dumb luck." Clowes recalls. Zwigoff's wife happened to be a fan of his work, particularly "Ghost World," as was underground comic book pioneer Robert Crumb, the subject of a previous film by Zwigoff. And film writing seems to suit Clowes.

Now, he's working on a screenplay that isn't based on one of his comics—a "biopic of sorts," Clowes explains, about "three guys who did an incredible shot-for-shot remake of 'Raiders of the Lost Ark,' taking up their entire adolescence from 1982 to 1989."

The three fellows—Eriz Zala, Jayson Lamb and Chris Strompolos—have enjoyed considerable coverage in the media. Even Steven Spielberg lauded them. The film on their obsessive project, with Clowes' script, is scheduled for a 2007 release.

"I think I've finally got the hang of it," he says, referring to the writing of a screenplay. "By this point, I think I can bend it to my will."

Life Drawing[*]

With a New Graphic Memoir, Cartoonist Alison Bechdel Proves She's More Than Just a Dyke to Watch Out For

By Margot Harrison
Seven Days (Burlington, Vt.), May 31–June 7, 2006

"People who write graphic novels are clinically insane," says Alison Bechdel. The Bolton [Vermont]-based cartoonist, author of the nationally syndicated cult strip "Dykes to Watch Out For" is referring to her new book, *Fun Home*, a memoir of family art and artifice told in words and pictures. The complex tale deals with homosexuality in two generations, suicide, classic literature and life in a rural Pennsylvania funeral home.

Fun Home is a departure for Bechdel. And the book has the potential to catapult her into the big time. A recent blurb in *Time* magazine called the book "brilliant" and "bleakly hilarious." Bechdel scheduled her interview with *Seven Days* around photo shoots with *People* and *Entertainment Weekly*. She's in the midst of a month-long national book tour.

"I'm actually kind of envious of myself, if that's possible," says Bechdel. "I'm used to feeling underrated and bitter, so I've had to do some gear-shifting. Now I'm worried about being overrated."

For most of her 23-year career, Bechdel didn't even have an agent. She handles her own syndication and published most of her 11 "Dykes to Watch Out For" compilations with Firebrand Books, a "one-woman publisher" in Ithaca, New York. In 2000, just as Bechdel was starting work on *Fun Home*, Firebrand ran into financial trouble and was sold off.

The resultant "turmoil" gave Bechdel the impetus to seek and find an agent, who, she says, "had much higher sights for my work than I did." The agent promptly sold the memoir proposal to Houghton Mifflin, which is pulling out all the stops to promote the book. Bechdel points out that *Fun Home* is the big-name publisher's first "graphic novel"—a hot genre in the multimedia age, and one that's finally getting critical respect. Technically, of course, it's not a novel but a memoir, which means it may also appeal to the readers who made *The Liars' Club* and *Angela's Ashes* into best sellers.

The publisher is probably also banking on the following Bechdel has developed through her comic strip. Since 1983, when "Dykes to Watch Out For" started as a set of single panels in a feminist newspaper in New York City, its audience has been steadily growing. Initially, the strip was a series of vignettes from urban lesbian life. In 1987, the strip began to read like a soap opera, if soap operas could be literate, lesbian and politically engaged. The true diversity of the characters, a matter not just of color and class but of ideology and temperament, kept sparks flying.

Bechdel's first book, a compilation of her cartoons, came out in 1986; she's since published 10 more that have collectively sold a quarter of a million copies. The combination of royalties, syndication and profits from "Dykes" merchandise—she used to ship calendars, mugs and mouse pads out of her three-story home—have sustained her since 1991, the year she moved to Vermont. Today, "Dykes" runs in 50 gay and alternative papers, including *Seven Days*. Back in the '90s, Universal Press Syndicate offered to carry "Dykes" if Bechdel would adapt it for more conservative audiences—starting by choosing a tamer title. She declined.

But what fails to fly on a daily paper's comics page may sell just fine on a bookshelf. *Fun Home* doesn't hold back on lesbian content—there's one fairly graphic sex scene. It doesn't hurt that Bechdel's skills as a writer and artist have earned her considerable cred in the comics world. She's garnered praise from underground comic legends like Harvey Pekar, of *American Splendor* fame, as well as their mainstream counterparts. Venerable Brookfield *New Yorker* cartoonist Ed Koren compares Bechdel to Garry Trudeau and calls "Dykes" "probably the best cultural strip around."

Most successful memoirs fall into the same general subject categories as episodes of *Dr. Phil*: Abuse, Addiction and Weird Families. While they can and often do offer complexity and catharsis unknown to daytime TV, they also appeal to our voyeuristic interest in other people's secrets.

Fun Home falls into the "weird family" category. The story pivots around Bechdel's father, about whom we learn two vital things in the first chapter. The first is that this respectable citizen of a rural Pennsylvania town, a high school English teacher and third-generation funeral director, had a secret life in which he slept with male students and his children's babysitter.

The second is that he stepped in front of a truck when he was 44 years old. While the townspeople chose to see his death as accidental, Bechdel—who was 19 at the time—strongly suspects that it was actually a suicide. Though he was a perfectionist, whose painstakingly restored Gothic revival house enabled him to posture like an Appalachian Jay Gatsby, Bruce Bechdel was a flawed and mysterious human being.

Besides the family secrets, the book offers an element of funeral-home chic. Fans of HBO's "Six Feet Under" may notice some similar motifs in *Fun Home*. The title is the Bechdel children's nickname for the family business, where their dad embalmed corpses when he wasn't teaching *Catcher in the Rye*. As in the TV series, there's a dead father, a gay child who comes out to the rest of the family, an imposing Victorian house and, of course, the corpses. When the show got big, Bechdel says her agent actually "wondered if somebody had overheard me telling my story in a coffee shop and lifted it."

That's pretty much where the parallels with "Six Feet Under" end. Rather than generating story lines, the dead folks here serve to emphasize the family's oddly detached approach to the world. In one sequence, Bechdel recalls her father showing her an opened corpse as if as a "test." "The emotion I had suppressed for the gaping cadaver seemed to stay suppressed," she writes. "Even when it was Dad himself on the prep table."

Fun Home is also a memoir of addiction, in a sense—"addiction" to creative pursuits and the hermetic and obsessive-compulsive tendencies that often accompany them. In one panel, Bechdel cross-sections her childhood home to reveal each member of the family absorbed in his or her solitary obsession—herself drawing, one brother making model airplanes and another strumming the guitar, her mother playing the piano, and her father indulging his passion for historical preservation.

"If our family was a sort of artists' colony, could it not be even more accurately described as a mildly autistic colony?" a subsequent caption asks. Though the book is set in the 1970s, it's an oddly resonant image in our age of wired families, where focused pursuits like IM-ing and blogging have replaced impromptu games of tag with the kids down the block.

The structure of the book may put off readers looking for a straightforward story. Having made her big "reveal" early on, Bechdel proceeds to shuttle back and forth in her memories, creating a complex, nonchronological narrative. We see young Alison "trying to compensate for something unmanly" in her father by embracing all things butch, long before she knows of his homosexuality. We see her in college, realizing with both joy and trepidation that she's a lesbian, and later we see her worrying that coming out to her father—an act almost unimaginable in his generation—might have had something to do with his death.

Meanwhile, Bechdel lards these narratives with parallels drawn from literary works, her favorites or her parents'. For instance, Proust's *Within a Budding Grove*, with its portrayal of pubescent girls and flowers as virtually indistinguishable, serves as an ironic counterpoint to her own "butch" youth. It's also a covertly gay romance, much like her father's life. Bechdel shows us how she saw her world as a child by reproducing the map from *The Wind in the Willows*. When her father finally and fleetingly opens up to her about his homosexuality, she compares this with a pivotal meeting of the artist and his "spiritual father" in Joyce's *Ulysses*.

In some writers' hands, this reliance on literary metaphors would get ponderous. Bechdel herself says she initially feared it would be "pretentious." But, in a family where life imitated fiction, and a father handed his daughter a Colette book rather than asking her whether she was a lesbian, the parallels make sense.

Besides, whenever the narrating voice at the top of the panel threatens to get too professorial, Bechdel's sly, intimate images of family life bring things back to earth.

As the narrator enumerates her father's similarities to F. Scott Fitzgerald, we see her younger self entering his baronial library and asking for a check to buy "some new *Mad* books." That dead-on detail of the '70s, combined with the simple transaction between father and daughter—"Write it out and I'll sign it," he says, absorbed in his own book—is touching on another level. It reminds us that "weird families" can be ordinary families, and vice versa. We wouldn't care about their dark secrets if we couldn't relate.

"I can't make things up. I have no imagination," says 45-year-old Bechdel. She's perched on an ergonomic chair in her basement studio. "But I can take real life and put it in a box," she goes on. "That's the thing I can do."

The windows of the studio frame intensely green foliage—the edge of 39 acres that Bechdel owns on a mountain road still soft and rutted from spring floods. Inside, the studio is an urban oasis of Macintoshes and graphic arts paraphernalia. A framed poster of Hergé's plucky comic book hero Tintin hangs on the wall. A 17-year-old tortoiseshell cat enters silently as a ghost.

Bechdel works here six days a week and saves all her Burlington errands for Wednesday, to "maximize efficiency," she says. Then there's the quintessentially rural routine of fetching her mail from the small-town Jonesville post office. Fans of "Dykes to Watch Out For" ask her, "'How do you write about these urban characters and this subculture when you don't really live in it?'" she says. "I couldn't work without the Internet. I can find out anything from my basement in Vermont." Research has grown especially important for Bechdel as she gives "Dykes" a "broader political mandate." In recent years, the strip has tackled gay marriage, parenting, the election and the various horror shows of America under the Bush administration.

While "Dykes" requires Bechdel to stay current, *Fun Home* sent her back into her past. "I've wanted to tell this story since I was about 20," Bechdel says, "as soon as I had enough perspective on my father's death to see what a really excellent story it was. For a long time I thought I couldn't reveal this family secret. But something changed along the way . . . history changed, the cultural climate changed, and eventually it didn't seem like that earthshaking a thing to reveal, even for my family."

When she first conceived the book about her father, Bechdel didn't realize she could draw the story. "When I was 20, there wasn't such a thing as a graphic novel," she says. *Maus*, Art Spiegelman's acclaimed graphic novel of the Holocaust, hadn't come out yet. "So that was part of the evolution, too," Bechdel says, "finding a form for the story to take. At some point it just became clear this was going to be a graphic narrative."

Creating *Fun Home* involved a more "labor-intensive process" than drawing the biweekly "Dykes" strip. Squatting on the floor, Bechdel rifles through crates in order to demonstrate the evolution of "one page from start to finish."

"The first thing I do is I write on the computer in a drawing program, which enables me to make these little text boxes and move them around, make my panel outlines," she says, fishing out a page of text that looks naked without images.

Next, Bechdel prints this framework and "starts doing very rough pencil sketches" on it. "Then I do several successive refinements of that sketch, and in doing that I take reference photos of myself, in the poses of all these characters," she says. She also does a "s---load of online research" to get backgrounds right—in this case, the rooftop of a particular building in Greenwich Village, from which Bechdel depicts her family watching the Bicentennial fireworks. Conveniently enough, the building is now a co-op with its own website. Like her father slaving over his historical renovations in *Fun Home*, Bechdel likes to nail down the details—"I can only deal with particulars," she says.

The next step is to put the refined sketch on a light box and trace it to the final drawing paper. The inked version is scanned back into the computer, where Bechdel fills in black areas using Adobe Photoshop, then combines her text and artwork files. In the last stage, she places the new print-out on the light box and shades it using an ink wash, creating a subtle two-color effect. "This page probably took me two days to create," she says. "I didn't even know how it was going to work out until I got the final book in my hand. It's quite a freakin' process."

Perhaps the most intriguing part of that process, for the layperson, is Bechdel's use of her digital camera to capture herself posing as the various people in the narrative. She says this technique was her response to an "utter failure of imagination." In promotional material, she describes herself as a "Method cartoonist."

Bechdel thinks her way of accessing the past demanded "a kind of weird acting ability. I was posing as my father, looking out at things as if I were my father." At one point she sought out the spot on the Pennsylvania highway where her father died. "I went and took a bunch of pictures as trucks were barrelling at me down the road," she says. "I had really gone just for the photo reference, but it had this added emotional kick, to give me the feeling of what it must have been like for my dad to be standing there making that decision to jump in front of a truck. If in fact that's what he did, which I'm not sure."

This scrupulousness is typical. Throughout the book, Bechdel speculates but also acknowledges the gaps in her understanding of her father's motivations. To recreate the past, she relied on "documentary evidence"—her father's letters, her childhood diaries and family photo albums she "commandeered."

In the wake of the James Frey debacle, there's been speculation about whether it's possible to write a compelling memoir without making things up. Bechdel admits that she filled in a few gaps with her imagination, sometimes inadvertently. Still, she says that "what I found was that [the evidence] was often much more interesting than anything I could possibly fabricate."

In a chapter called "The Ideal Husband," Bechdel describes a cluster of unsettling events that converged in the summer of 1974: her first period, Nixon's resignation, a plague of locusts, her father's run-in with the law for giving alcohol to a minor. "I had all these memories . . . but when I looked in my diary, I found that all these things had happened in a two-month period," she says. "If you were making that up, it would be really bad writing."

When she started *Fun Home*, Bechdel lacked confidence in herself as a writer. "I'm used to writing the comic strip, which is 90 percent dialogue. I had to learn to write," she says. It didn't help that both her parents were English teachers with "very refined tastes. I always felt both my parents looking over my shoulder as I was writing," she explains, "and it took a long time to shut them up and to trust that what I was doing was ok."

In *Fun Home*, Bechdel's narrator is a major presence. Occasionally there's a touch of glibness, as when she says, "My father's life was a solipsistic circle of self, from autocrat to autodidact to autocide." In general, though, the narrator's speculations are more intriguing than intrusive, because they heighten the force of the images.

When it came to those images, Bechdel was on surer footing. Based on "Dykes," Koren calls her "first-rate as an artist. She has a wonderful sense of detail and structure, putting together the dynamic of the strip," he says. "It's in the tradition of the grand old masters of cartoon strips. Just the way she uses blacks and whites and texture, the way her balloons flow across the page and divide the scene. There's a great sense of editing, going from long shot to close-up and back again."

James Sturm, director of the Institute for Cartoon Studies in White River Junction, says Bechdel has an "unfussy line that seems to perfectly relay an emotion or a gesture."

Panels in "Dykes to Watch Out For" tend to be multilayered—as in classic *Mad* magazines, you miss half the jokes if you don't read the characters' T-shirts or the headlines on newspapers they're carrying. "Some of my panels are friggin' illegible 'cause I'm trying to cram so much stuff in," Bechdel says. The larger format of *Fun Home* allowed her to use more empty space and also more "cinematic" techniques. For instance, a sudden "cut" from a side view of Alison and her father working on the lawn to a view from above underlines the distance between them, shifting the tone of the images abruptly from banality to elegy.

"All the time I've been working on this project, I've been operating under the assumption that it would be just like my 'Dykes' stuff—that is, that hardly anyone would ever see it," Bechdel says. Houghton Mifflin has a different plan. The publicity push for the book may imply that serious readers are finally embracing graphic novels—or memoirs, or whatever—as a legitimate form of literature. True to form, Bechdel counters, "People still can't stop themselves from saying, 'It's almost like a literary work!' When people are able to stop doing that, we will have arrived."

How has her family received *Fun Home*? Bechdel says her mother is having a "paradoxical reaction . . . She's never been keen on the idea that I was writing the book—she's very private, and even her closest friends don't know a lot of the stuff I reveal about my dad. Yet, oddly, she's psyched about the publicity. She told me she went into a bookstore the other day and bragged to the clerk about me."

While it will draw those inevitable comparisons to "Six Feet Under," *Fun Home* isn't just a tragicomic saga of a family living cheek by jowl with death. It's also a double coming-out story and what literary critics call a Künstlerroman—the story of how an artist came to be.

"I don't live in other worlds the way I used to," Bechdel says, contrasting her childhood of voracious reading with her more focused adulthood. "I've gone from living through other people's books to living through my own creative work." For all his perfectionism, her father surely would have approved.

Never Mind the Mullahs[*]

Iranian Exile Marjane Satrapi

By Vivienne Walt
Mother Jones, January/February 2008

Marjane Satrapi's autobiographical graphic novel *Persepolis* depicts Iran's recent history through the saucer eyes of a feisty girl whose childhood is upended by the 1979 Islamic revolution. At first, nine-year-old Marji is thrilled by the tumult around her, but as she enters adolescence she chafes under the restrictions of the new regime. Between art classes where chador-clad women pose as models, the teenage Satrapi and her friends secretly flirt, smoke dope, and swig homemade wine. You gotta love this girl: After convincing the fearsome female morality police not to lock her up for wearing a punk-rock jacket and a Michael Jackson button, she sneaks home, rips off her head scarf, and plays air guitar to a clandestine rock cassette. *Persepolis'* irreverence and acerbic wit made Satrapi a cult heroine among reformist Iranians and readers worldwide. One reviewer described her as "the Persian love child of [Art] Spiegelman and Lynda Barry."

Now living in self-imposed exile in Paris, the 38-year-old cartoonist has produced an animated version of her memoir. The movie won the 2007 Cannes Film Festival Jury Prize and packed theaters in Europe. An English version, featuring honey-voiced Catherine Deneuve as Satrapi's mother, Sean Penn as her father, and Iggy Pop as her uncle, has just been released in the States. It's likely to win her even more fans here, reinforcing her belief that the "Great Satan" and its foe in Tehran actually have a lot in common. When more Americans realize that, she says, "It becomes very hard to drop bombs on our heads."

Mother Jones: Iran protested that *Persepolis* was included at Cannes. I understand you stay out of Iran completely these days.

Marjane Satrapi: It is not as if they have sent me letters saying, "If you come back we will do this or that to you." But I don't know what will happen, and so I don't go back.

MJ: Are you still attached to the country?

MS: I have a couple of friends who are Iranian, but I don't think we can call that a community. I have family in Iran, but I don't talk very much about the situation in Iran today because whatever I know is secondhand information. The image that I have of Iran today is mixed so much with my melancholy and my nostalgia that I can't have a fair point of view.

MJ: What would take you back to Iran?

MS: The day we have a democracy, I will probably go back to Iran.

MJ: What do you imagine your life would be like had you never left?

MS: [Laughs.] Maybe I would have been happier. I'm a very individualistic person. That is why I don't belong to any political party or anything. I really believe in justice and freedom. I felt it was better for me to leave, given the person I was.

MJ: From a young age you were a little firebrand. What gave you that courage?

MS: My mother was the favorite child of her parents. My father was the favorite child of his parents. The result of these two favorite children was me. And I am an only child. So I was convinced that I was the center of the universe.

MJ: As a teenager in Iran, did you really have a jacket that said, "Punk is Not Ded," as you do in the movie?

MS: Yes, but it did not have "Punk is Not Ded." What was written on it was something else. I won't tell you what—that is the secret part of my life!

MJ: Did you really have a Michael Jackson button?

MS: Oh, yes. I got arrested for that button. But let us not talk about what is true and what is not true. You liked the movie, and that is important.

MJ: Your parents sent you off to school in Europe when you were 14. Why did you leave Iran the second time?

MS: It was due to many things—my unhappy marriage and all that. But also I wanted to do my artistic work, and in Iran you have censorship. It was difficult for me to do the work I wanted to do.

MJ: What led you to create *Persepolis*?

MS: I'd heard so many stupidities about my country since I left Iran. People had watched this stupid movie *Not Without My Daughter* [in which Sally Field plays an American who rescues her daughter from her estranged in-laws in Iran]; I heard so many things like that. I did not make *Persepolis* for Iranians. It was my answer to the rest of the world, to say, "Let me give you another point of view."

MJ: Is there a reason why this had to be a graphic novel?

MS: Writing is not for me. I completely lose my sense of humor when I write. I become extremely pathetic, very sensational. Images give me possibilities that I don't have with words.

MJ: How do you feel about the enormous response to *Persepolis?*

MS: I became the voice of a generation in a very surprising way, because many Iranians recognize themselves in it. But that is not what I wanted. I don't like the word "autobiography." I rather like the term "autofiction." The second you make a script out of the story of your life, it becomes fictional. Of course, the truth is never far. But the story is created out of it.

MJ: You have said that Darth Vader was the *Star Wars* character you most wanted to be.

MS: Absolutely. I was in love with Darth Vader. He was extremely sexy to me. About five years ago, I had almost a sexual dream about Darth Vader. At the moment he was about to pull his helmet off, my husband woke me up and I was so annoyed. I told him, "I was on my way to kiss Darth Vader."

MJ: What do you make of the fact that you are so popular among Americans?

MS: I'm very happy about it. The U.S. is threatening Iran, and then here is this Iranian whom they love. There is no problem between people; the problem is on the political side.

MJ: Likewise, I am always amazed how many people in Iran have read the latest books coming out of the States, or have relatives in L.A., and so on.

MS: Absolutely. I think the most pro-Western country in that region is Iran. The government, no. But the people love Westerners.

Cartoon Politics[*]

By Michael Scott Leonard
The Berkshire Eagle (Mass.), November 14, 2007

I first became aware of graphic novels about four or five years ago, around the time they began to enter the public consciousness through film adaptations and the reluctantly glowing reviews of established literary outlets. Like most Americans, I was late to the party.

Though graphic novels have appeared on the mainstream's radar only within the last few years, comic books with serious artistic ambition date back to the underground comics movement of the 1960s and '70s. Like any literary or artistic movement, the form has matured over the years and decades, developing stylistic and narrative conventions all its own and becoming increasingly gentrified. Before crashing the gates of the literary world, graphic novels enjoyed a dedicated but decidedly cultish following. Their appeal is now considerably broader, with the Gray Lady herself (The New York Times) designating Allison Bechdel's graphic memoir, "Fun Home: A Family Tragicomic," one of its "100 Notable Books of the Year" for 2006.

To commemorate the graphic novel's coming of age, the Norman Rockwell Museum opened "LitGraphic: The Art of the Graphic Novel," an exhibition featuring the work of 24 acclaimed graphic novelists, last week. One of the artists, Howard Cruse, is a North Adams resident whose 1995 graphic novel, "Stuck Rubber Baby," won a number of prestigious comic art awards and was nominated for the American Library Association's Lesbian and Gay Book Award.

Cruse, the son of an Alabama preacher, got his start cartooning for The Baptist Student while still in high school. Like many people at the time, he considered comics and cartoons the purview of political satirists and juvenile doodlers, but his parents encouraged his burgeoning talents.

"When I was young, my ambition was to draw a comic strip, and both Mom and Dad were really supportive," he told me during a recent telephone interview.

"Dad, in particular, encouraged me, because he sort of wished he could have been more artistic himself. But he got diverted into other things."

Cruse attended Birmingham-Southern College, leaving behind what he began to see as a childish hobby. "I had a sense, as many people do, that to be a cartoonist meant that you couldn't bring the kinds of serious artistic issues into your work that a novelist or a playwright could," he said. "It was seen as a sort of juvenile medium, and I had become very serious about my art from working in theater during college, so I had gotten away from thinking of myself as headed for a cartooning career."

It wasn't until he earned a degree in drama and encountered the underground comics movement that he began to synthesize his cartooning prowess with the emotional resonance of more traditional art forms.

"After I finished college and the underground comics movement started, I realized I would be able to bring my seriousness about art—by which I mean exploring the substantive issues of life, not a lack of humor—that I could do that through my cartooning," he said.

These artistic epiphanies were not occurring in a vacuum, of course—they never do. Around the same time, Cruse was coming to terms with his homosexuality, which, as a preacher's son in the pre-gay liberation South, he had long repressed. He came out of the closet not long after college, but he didn't begin incorporating his sexual orientation into his work until the late 1970s.

"I realized pretty early in the '70s that I ultimately wanted to be openly gay professionally, but I was also becoming open about a lot of different aspects of life—about all the big issues of life and death and politics and religion," he told me. "I did comics for several years before I explicitly came out, partly because I wanted to establish myself as an artist with my reputation not totally hinging on (my) being the 'gay artist.'

"If you're serious about being an artist, one of the main factors at play is how honest you're willing to be about your inner life," he added. "I think art becomes more powerful the more the audience senses that what they're seeing is authenticity, not artifice."

And how did the preacher father take the gay cartoonist son's lifestyle?

"My dad died when I was in college, before I began doing gay-related stuff," Cruse said. "Dad wasn't a stereotypical Alabama preacher. He was, in his way, an intellectual, and he might have come around; he changed his attitude about a number of social issues at the time, but he never got a chance to be tested on that score. My mother's always been great about it."

The Rockwell exhibit, which runs through May 26, 2008, represents a coming-out party of a different sort. There may be no more iconic American painter than Norman Rockwell. A celebration of the graphic novel by the museum to which he gives his name validates the form's maturation and growing cultural prominence.

"Every now and then, someone will put together a show with a theme like this, and that's an outgrowth of the fact that graphic novels are now treated as serious literature," said Cruse. "The New York Times began reviewing graphic novels a few years ago, which was a big step—when mine came out, I couldn't get The Times to review it.

"There are a lot of ways in which the gatekeepers make decisions for the public about what constitutes serious art and what doesn't. Last year, finally, a number of graphic novels got major play in magazines. So we're having lots of breakthroughs, and with that comes shows like they're doing at the Rockwell."

Cruse's contribution to the exhibition is a brief excerpt—"a number of pretty much consecutive pages"—from "Stuck Rubber Baby," a book that chronicles his "experience of the gay subculture as it existed in a Southern city before most people were aware of a serious gay liberation movement . . . and a young man's struggle with taking responsibility for his actions at a time when white Southerners were being challenged about how much they were going to put on the line for racial integration."

"This is just one incident in the story," he said. "It's not specifically about gay rights or civil rights; it's just an amusing incident based on an anecdote I heard while researching the novel. I put it in the book because it was irresistible. It was so outrageous, but it was true, and I thought, 'These kind of anecdotes don't along come every day.'"

Neither does this kind of exhibition.

CR Sunday Interview[*]

Gene Luen Yang

By Tom Spurgeon
The Comics Reporter, June 20, 2010

It's been only a few years since Gene Luen Yang roared to a kind of cartooning success emblematic of new ways of fashioning a comics career. His *American Born Chinese* became the first graphic novel to receive a nomination for a National Book Award (in the young people's literature category). The book would go on to win the ALA's Michael L. Printz award for young-adult literature, another first. It also sold like the dickens throughout. I don't know anyone who didn't root for Yang when he was picking up the honors, and I know few people interested in the world of comics that haven't tracked his attempts to build on that rush of success since.

Yang followed up *American Born Chinese* with the more difficult, complex, short-story collection *The Eternal Smile* (with friend and fellow major talent Derek Kirk Kim), and now *Prime Baby*, which was the last feature to appear in the *New York Times*' run of comics in its Sunday Magazine. I thought *Prime Baby* very charming when I picked up the recent collection, and took the chance to contact Yang so we could maybe go back and forth a bit. I'm glad he agreed.

TOM SPURGEON: *I don't want to give you as impossibly as broad a first question as how* American Born Chinese *might have changed your life, but I wonder how such a big and obvious success on the resume might have had an impact on the way you work. Was there any time at all where it might have felt like a hindrance to work under that book's considerable shadow? Do you feel like there are expectations for your work that might not be been there before?*

GENE LUEN YANG: Well, there are expectations in that more than my mom and my cartoonist friends read my comics now. To be honest, I do feel some pressure. I think a lot of it comes from the advance system that the book industry uses, that the comics industry is slowly adopting. Not to complain about the money that a publisher is willing to invest in me, but with money comes pressure. If you make a sucky mini-comic, nothing really prevents you from making your next mini-comic. If I lose a lot of money for my publisher, I don't know . . . I can't imagine them wanting to continue giving me advances.

Practically speaking, the success of *American Born Chinese* has allowed me to devote more time to making comics. I've been able to go part-time at my day job, so I get 2–3 full days each week at my drawing table. I used to have to do comics in the early morning, at night, and on the weekends.

SPURGEON: *For that matter, have you been able to fully enjoy that book's success, do you think? Now that you've had a couple of years, is there anything about the experience in terms of how well that book did that stands out to you?*

YANG: Sure, I've been able to fully enjoy the success of *American Born Chinese*. I got to go to Angouleme with my French-speaking editor Mark Seigel. I got to go to Washington D.C. for the National Book Festival. I got to serve as a judge for the National Book Awards last year. I got to be a special guest at Comic-Con. I got to shake Neil Gaiman's hand when I accepted the Eisner. If you told me five years ago that *American Born Chinese* would result in any one of these things, I would've laughed myself silly. But for all of them to happen? It's so amazing that it almost feels like some kind of practical joke.

I remember being really worried right before my panel at Comic-Con that no one was going to show up. It's happened before at book signings and such. I did this one at my local Borders after the NBA nomination that was like that. The staff were really nice. They put out this coffee/frosty/smoothie-type drink in little sampler cups on my table, and they had a beautiful display of my books in the corner. One person came up to talk to me. Nobody asked me to sign. Several people waited until I wasn't looking in their direction to sneak a sampler cup.

But the Comic-Con panel was totally different. People showed up. A lot more people than I expected. They asked great questions and seemed genuinely interested in my comics. An experience that stands out? That was probably it.

SPURGEON: *You probably did the healthiest thing available to you as a same-publisher follow-up to ABC in that* The Eternal Smile *was almost radically different—in fact, the short stories in that book all break in different directions from each other, let alone from past work. Was that a satisfying work to put together, these different stories in different modes and with different tones, all in color, after such a sustained graphic novel effort? It looked like you guys were having fun but at the same time I could also see the book as being laborious in terms of its execution.*

YANG: We were having fun. Eh. I should say, I was having fun. It was laborious, but Derek was the one providing all the labor. All I had to do was send him a script and then wait for these incredible pages to show up in my inbox.

Derek is one of my closest friends, so working with him is always fun. "Duncan's Kingdom," the first story in *The Eternal Smile*, was originally published by Image Comics in the late '90s as a two-issue mini-series. At the time, Derek was going through a bout of writer's block. He told me he wanted to draw some fantasy-type stuff, but couldn't think of a story. He asked me to write for him and I jumped at the chance.

We both eventually moved on to our own projects, but "Duncan's Kingdom" had a special place in our hearts. When we got hooked up with First Second, we wanted to collect "Duncan," but it was too short to stand on its own. We fleshed it out with two more stories dealing with the same theme and ended up with *The Eternal Smile*.

I'm very proud of the work for the reasons you mentioned. It's the most beautiful book I've ever worked on, mostly because Derek handled all the visuals. I got to experiment with different writing voices because I knew Derek's art could embody the differences in a way that my own art could not. He really did an amazing job.

SPURGEON: *There are what I would say are obvious cautionary elements to* The Eternal Smile *in terms of how it presents fantasy vis-a-vis reality. What I couldn't tell— and maybe you don't want to tell—is where your personal sympathies lie. Is it enough to pick up a kind of critical ethos to the stories in that book, or is there a specific criticism of fantasy and its limits you'd like the reader to consider?*

YANG: I think "Duncan's Kingdom" is particularly anti-fantasy. I'm a geek and I've certainly consumed more than my fair share of fantasy pop culture. "Duncan's Kingdom" might've been the result of geek self-loathing, that feeling you get after you've missed four consecutive meals because of videogames or when you realize that for the amount of money you spent on comics you could've bought a decent car.

As I've gotten older and less involved in fantasy pop culture as a consumer, I've softened in my self-loathing. Years ago, I had a student in one of my programming classes who never said a word. Whenever I asked him a question, he would look down at his feet and mumble. I used to keep the computer lab open after school, and this kid would come in regularly to work on his projects. We started talking.

I remember the conversation when he lost his mumble. He told me that he played one of those online fantasy games, World of Warcraft or EverQuest or something like that. Supposedly, in that game he was The Man. He was awesome at killing dragons or whatever, and he ran a guild that was made up of players who were much older than him, 20- and 30-somethings. When he talked about that game, he got this confidence in his voice that I hadn't heard before. He became a guild leader. He became The Man.

That was my first real experience of one of those benefits of fantasy culture that fantasy apologists are always talking about. But it's true. Those leadership skills and that confidence were always in my student. It just took a videogame to bring it out. As he got older, more and more of his dragon-killing guild-leader self emerged in his real life.

I see that a lot as a teacher. A lot of students find their confidence in some sort of subculture. Maybe it's anime club or a sports team or some sort of virtual environment. They find their voice there, and as they get older they learn to bridge the gap between that subculture and the wider world. They bring their confident alias out into the open.

That was in the back of my mind when I was writing "Urgent Request."

SPURGEON: *I'm really fascinated by the use of white space in "Urgent Request." Supposing that was your contribution, is there a thematic component in terms of the isolation the character feels, or were you perhaps more interested in how that imagery floating in space read? How cognizant are you of page design and the quality of the experience of reading that you're offering an audience?*

YANG: Man, I wish I could take credit for that, but the white space was all Derek. I write in thumbnails, and the script I gave him was basically laid out on six-panel grids. He told me he wanted to try out this technique that was inspired by Chester Brown, where he'd draw all the panels first and then lay them out on the pages. He thought it would make for more controlled pacing. He was right. In that story, the white space becomes a part of the storytelling voice.

SPURGEON: *I want to make sure to ask a bunch of questions about* Prime Baby, *which is the book that made me send you an e-mail. First of all, this was one of the* New York Times *Sunday Magazine Funny Pages comics, the last one if I'm not mistaken. I don't know anything about how that project worked. How were you contacted? How much editorial back and forth was there between that time and when the work began to be printed? Did you enjoy the process of making the book?*

YANG: Yep, it was the last one. They canceled the feature after my story finished.

The *New York Times* contacted my agent, my agent asked me, and I said yes because, you know, it's THE NEW YORK FREAKING TIMES. There was some editorial back and forth in the beginning. I proposed one or two story ideas that they didn't think was appropriate for the paper before landing on *Prime Baby*. Originally, I wanted to do a story about a porn addict who is visited by leprechauns.

SPURGEON: *[laughs] So what ended up being your interest in doing* Prime Baby *for this gig? Was this a story you'd been thinking about doing or is this something that was more of a direct response to the specific publishing opportunity?*

YANG: *Prime Baby* was a direct response to the *New York Times* gig. It came from three different sources. First, my wife and I had recently had our second child and we were dealing with sibling rivalry at home. Second, I assign this prime numbers exercise to my programming students every year, and they often ask what the point of prime numbers is. Finally, I wrote this short story a couple of years ago about a baby who spoke in prime numbers. I used to do 15 minute free-writes as a way to warm up before scripting something, and the short story was the result of one of those free-writes.

SPURGEON: *Were you aware of what other cartoonists had done in the series by the time you were working on* Prime Baby? *Was* Prime Baby *in any way a reaction to what had previously been published?*

YANG: I'd read both Jason's and Seth's stories. *Prime Baby* wasn't a conscious reaction to them, but I felt very, very intimated about being in a space they'd once occupied. They're very different from each other, but they're both so polished, you know? And they both have these deep, [affecting] storytelling voices. Actually, maybe the "lightness" of *Prime Baby* was a reaction to them. I knew I couldn't compete in the same ballpark.

SPURGEON: *You mention lightness . . . I think more than any of the other comics that ran in the Times, yours was humorous in a way that we think of comic strips being humorous: was that intentional? Are you a strip fan, is that a mode of expression that you enjoyed inhabiting for a while? Were the constraints of the strip useful to you as a creator in any way?*

YANG: I love comic strips the way the vast majority of people love comic strips. I read them whenever I can. I have a couple of collections of *Calvin and Hobbes* at home. I just don't obsess over them like I do long-form comics.

I realized long ago that I am not a strip cartoonist. I can't handle the pressure of having to be funny every three panels.

That said, I do rely heavily on the rhythm of the page turn when I write comics. I try to have something that entices the reader to turn each page, maybe a question to be answered or a mild punchline. My love for the page turn is why I'm reluctant to do Scott McCloud's Infinite Canvas thing, despite being a computer nerd and very McCloudian in my thinking about comics.

Doing a comic for the *New York Times* was difficult. Those were the most constraints I'd ever had on a project. Each page had to essentially function as a chapter, and I had to have between 18 and 20 chapters, no more and no less. I learned a lot from that project, and I have renewed respect for cartoonists working in formats that are determined by someone other than themselves.

SPURGEON: *In collected form,* Prime Baby *has this sort of bouncy energy that makes it hard to remember that it was ever serialized. Was it hard for you at all to maintain what you were doing over the life a serial strip, even a relative short serial like this one?*

YANG: Some of the pages are definitely bouncier than others. I guess that's true of any work. Thaddeus's voice was pretty loud in my head, so coming up with all the jerk-ish dialog wasn't hard. Getting everything to fit into an 8" x 8" square was.

SPURGEON: *Is there anything to the way you construct the individual pages that's important on a project like this one? For instance, is it important that every individual story segment have a certain sort of gag, or that certain characters are voiced every time out? What is the intended effect of so much dropped detail in your panels, how so much of* Prime Baby *takes place against a single-color background?*

YANG: I have a pretty simple style to begin with, but the visuals of *Prime Baby* are especially simplistic. I drew dots for the eyes and very few background details. All those decisions were a response to the limited space. Thaddeus is a pretty wordy kid, at least in his own thoughts, so the pages would already be crowded with text.

I was worried that competing details in the images would be off-putting to the reader, so I simplified even more than I normally do.

SPURGEON: *How much sympathy do you have for Thaddeus? He's a comically dis-agreeable character in a lot of obvious ways, but you're also upfront about him working from these positions of real pain and fear. Plus it ends up he's largely right.*

YANG: Derek tells me that of all my characters, Thaddeus is most like me in real life. I'm not sure how to take that. I tried to build sympathy for Thaddeus, both in my reader and myself, by making him relatively young. When a third grader suggests that his baby sister needs to be dissected, it's kind of funny. If a sixth grader were to do it, you'd want to call in the professionals.

I do like him a lot. As I said before, his voice is very clear to me. I hope to use him again in a future project. I've been batting around a couple of ideas in the back of my head as I've worked on my other stuff, but I don't have anything concrete yet.

SPURGEON: *Is it fair to see the strip as critical of a certain kind of parenting? The parents seem to accept Thaddeus' apparent similar state a bit too quickly for me.*

YANG: Yes, it's fair. I think modern parents are encouraged to over-parent in this very . . . I don't know . . . *chic* way that tries to hide the real difficulty of parenting. I'm particularly susceptible to over-parenting because I tend towards paranoia, especially where my kids are concerned. I feel the pressure to read the latest studies on nap time and buy the latest BPA-free bottles and install the latest organic car seats.

But you can do all this stuff and still find that a grumpy baby is a pain in the butt. New technology doesn't relieve parents of the hardest parts of parenting, but as modern people we sort of expect it to.

Thaddeus's parents are a send-up of modern parents. I don't know how much of it comes through the final pages of *Prime Baby*, but I definitely had all this in mind when I was writing those two characters.

SPURGEON: *The Sunday Times Magazine was a humongous platform for any comics work. Did you hear back from people as the comic was serialized? Did what you hear have any effect on how you presented the print collection?*

YANG: I did hear back from some folks. There were some prime number fans who wrote me, and some parents of kids named Thaddeus. It was pretty much all positive feedback. I suspect that the folks who didn't like it were not passionate enough in their dislike to write me about it. That has not been true for my other comics.

Reader feedback didn't really have an effect on the print collection at all. The presentation of the print collection was designed by First Second, with some input from me. They did an amazing job, in my opinion.

SPURGEON: *Has anyone blamed you for killing that feature, Gene?*

YANG: I asked the *Times* folks over and over again about this and they've assured me that it's not my fault. But I have my doubts. Thanks for bringing it up, Tom.

SPURGEON: *Your Airbender boycott: were you comfortable using your comics-making skills in that fashion? I thought that mode of presentation really suited your style, but I wondered if you felt that way. When you do a comic like that, do you think in terms of changing minds or is it more about the personal satisfaction of staking out a position that important to you, no matter what others think? How controlled a piece of rhetoric is that comic?*

YANG: For that one I used my teacher-self (which is basically me doing my best Scott McCoud impression) because the strip is about teaching rather than arguing. I wanted to raise awareness about a particular issue without beating the reader over the head with it. Righteous indignation is really, really fun, but there's just too much of it these days, you know? I wanted to share my line of thinking while respecting the reader's decisions and free will.

SPURGEON: *Gene, I have no idea what you have coming up in future months. Is there a next major project?*

YANG: I've got a few things in the works. Early next year, First Second will be releasing a graphic novel I did with Thien Pham, a fellow Bay Area cartoonist. Thien is actually one of three cartoonists teaching at my school, so we see each other pretty regularly. (Brianna Miller is the third.) Our project is called *Level Up*, and it's about a videogame freak who gets a divine calling to go to med school. I handled the writing and he handled the art. This one has been a long time coming. It was originally called *Three Angels* and slated to come out the year after *American Born Chinese*, but the story was sucky so we redid it. I've written more drafts of this story than any of my other ones. After *American Born Chinese* started getting some attention, I freaked out a little bit because I realized that I'd been constructing my stories on pure instinct. I never really understood story structure. So I read a bunch of books on story and plot and character and wrote *Three Angels*. It was a stiff and terrible thing. I'm much happier with *Level Up*.

I've also been working on a historical fiction project about the Boxer Rebellion in late 19th Century China. In the early 2000s, Pope John Paul II canonized a couple hundred Chinese saints. These were the first Chinese ever to be canonized by the Catholic Church. The church I grew up in, a Chinese Catholic Church in the South Bay, made a big deal out of this, naturally.

I looked into these saints and discovered that many of them were martyred during the Boxer Rebellion. These Chinese Catholics were killed by the Boxers— poor Chinese peasant boys who were angry at the European presence in China— because the Chinese Catholics were seen as traitors to their own people for embracing a foreign faith. The Communist government in China actually protested the canonizations on these grounds.

I found that this historical conflict embodied a conflict Chinese and Asian Christians sometimes feel between our cultural heritage and our faith. As I read more about both the Boxers and the Chinese Christians, I became less and less clear about who to root for. So that's what this project is about. It will be two different graphic novels. The first will feature the Boxers as the protagonists and the second the Chinese Christians. There will be shared characters. I'm writing and drawing everything myself, and Lark Pien has agreed to color it. I've already been working on it for a couple of years. I'm about 3/4 of the way through the first volume. It's just taking forever.

Finally, I've been invited to contribute to the next volume of *Strange Tales* from Marvel Comics. I'm really excited about that. I'm doing a short four-pager for that.

Bibliography

Books

Bitz, Michael. *Manga High: Literacy, Identity, and Coming of Age in an Urban High School.* Cambridge, Mass.: Harvard Education Press, 2009.

Brenner, Robin. *Understanding Manga and Anime.* Santa Barbara, Calif.: Libraries Unlimited, 2007.

Carter, James Bucky, ed. *Building Literacy Connections with Graphic Novels: Page by Page, Panel by Panel.* Urbana, Ill.: National Council of Teachers of English, 2007.

Cary, Stephen. *Going Graphic: Comics at Work in the Multilingual Classroom.* Portsmouth, N.H.: Heinemann, 2004.

Cornog, Martha, and Timothy Perper, eds. *Graphic Novels: Beyond the Basics: Insights and Issues for Libraries.* Santa Barbara, Calif.: Libraries Unlimited, 2009.

Crawford, Philip Charles. *Graphic Novels 101: Selecting and Using Graphic Novels to Promote Literacy for Children and Young Adults: A Resource Guide for School Librarians and Educators.* Spring, Tex.: Hi Willow Research and Publishing, 2003.

Goldsmith, Francisca. *Graphic Novels Now: Building, Managing, and Marketing a Dynamic Collection.* Chicago: ALA Editions, 2005.

————. *The Reader's Advisory Guide to Graphic Novels.* Chicago, Ill.: ALA Editions, 2009.

Gorman, Michele. *Getting Graphic! Using Graphic Novels to Promote Literacy with Preteens and Teens.* Santa Barbara, Calif.: Linworth Publishing, Inc., 2003.

————. *Getting Graphic! Comics for Kids.* Santa Barbara, Calif.: Linworth Publishing, Inc., 2008.

Lyga, Allyson A. W., and Barry Lyga. *Graphic Novels in Your Media Center: A Definitive Guide.* Santa Barbara, Calif.: Libraries Unlimited, 2004.

Miller, Steve. *Developing and Promoting Graphic Novel Collections.* New York: Neal-Schuman Publishers, 2005.

Pawuk, Michael. *Graphic Novels: A Genre Guide to Comic Books, Manga, and More.* Santa Barbara, Calif.: Libraries Unlimited, 2006.

Serchay, David S. *The Librarian's Guide to Graphic Novels for Children and Tweens.* New York: Neal-Schuman Publishers, 2008.

———. *The Librarian's Guide to Graphic Novels for Adults.* New York: Neal-Schuman Publishers, 2010.

Thompson, Jason. *Manga: The Complete Guide.* New York: Del Rey Manga, 2007.

Pendergast, Tom, and Sara Pendergast, eds. *U X L Graphic Novelists.* Farmington Hills, Mich.: Thomson Gale, 2006.

Weiner, Robert G., ed. *Graphic Novels and Comics in Libraries and Archives: Essays on Readers, Research, History and Cataloging.* Jefferson, N.C.: McFarland, 2010.

Weiner, Stephen. *101 Best Graphic Novels.* New York: NBM, 2005.

———. *The Rise of the Graphic Novel: Faster Than a Speeding Bullet.* New York: NBM Publishing, 2003.

Web Sites

Readers seeking additional information on graphic novels, comic books, and related subjects may wish to consult the following Web sites, all of which were operational as of this writing.

The Beat

http://www.comicsbeat.com

The Beat "is dedicated to providing the timeliest and most pertinent news and information about comics, the people who make them, the readers who love them and the world that shapes them." Launched and maintained by editor-in-chief Heidi MacDonald, an award-winning writer and journalist, The Beat is updated at least daily and includes a variety of informative content, from news reports and commentary to videos and links.

Comic Book Resources (CBR)

http://www.comicbookresources.com

Serving over 3.8 million visitors each month, this Web site describes itself as "the premiere online comics magazine." Users can access blogs, reviews, and weekly columns, as well as daily features that provide up-to-the-minute news about comics and such comics-related media as movies and television programs.

COMICON.com Pulse

http://www.comicon.com/pulse

This Web site, associated with COMICON.com, "The World's Biggest Comic Book Convention," includes news and interviews, information on comics-related events, and a range of other material. Specific sections focus on such topics as "Comics Culture," "Comics Tech," and "Comics and Graphic Novels."

Comics Bulletin

http://www.comicsbulletin.com

Comics Bulletin describes itself as "The Internet's Most Diverse Comic Webzine." Visitors can find opinion and gossip columns, reviews of comics issues and trade paperbacks, interviews, interactive forums, and other helpful material.

Comics in the Classroom

http://comicsintheclassroom.net

This Web site includes links to lesson plans, reviews, news, essays, and interviews with comics creators. Visitors can access special features, including Jason Thompson's overview of the manga genre for children and teenagers and reviews, by Tracy Edmunds and her two daughters, of recommended titles.

Comics Reporter

http://www.comicsreporter.com

This award-winning Web site, which debuted in 2004, is the brainchild of Tom Spurgeon, a renowned comic historian, author, and journalist. Spurgeon updates the site daily and blogs regularly on comics, graphic novels, and related subjects. He provides links to interesting articles and blogs, which can keep visitors on the site for hours at a time.

Comics Worth Reading

http://comicsworthreading.com

Johanna Draper Carlson and Ed Sizemore share reviewing duties on this site. They cover graphic novels, comic books, manga, movies, television, and DVDs. They also provide cogent commentary on various issues affecting the comics industry.

Graphic Novel Reporter

http://www.graphicnovelreporter.com

This Web site, part of the Bookreporter.com network, includes reviews, interviews, polls, and other useful information about graphic novels. Also featured is a blog with posts by comics expert John Hogan and other contributors.

Kids Love Comics

http://www.kidslovecomics.com

Kids Love Comics is a nonprofit organization headed by comics creators, including Jimmy Gownley, John Gallagher, and Jane Smith Fisher; among its other members are educators and journalists. The group's mission is to increase awareness and interest in kids' comics. The organization's Web site includes podcasts, news articles, a list of recommended titles, and other helpful content.

Newsarama

http://www.newsarama.com

Since its launch in 1998, Newsarama.com has been "the source of choice for fans to find the latest news about the comic book industry, and animation, science fiction and fantasy entertainment on the big screen and on TV." In addition to news reports, columns, and interviews, Newsarama includes videos and other multimedia content.

No Flying, No Tights—Graphic Novel Reviews for Teens

http://www.noflyingnotights.com

Robin Brenner began writing about graphic novels on a Web site she created for a library school class. Now everyone can access her reviews and opinions on this colorful and fun Web site. Robin features a special section geared toward younger readers.

School Library Journal: Good Comics for Kids

http://blog.schoollibraryjournal.com/goodcomicsforkids

This is a team blog devoted to comics and graphic novels for children and teens. Managed by Brigid Alverson, the blog includes such members/posters as Robin Brenner. It is updated on an almost daily basis and includes reviews, commentary, interviews with comics creators, links to helpful Web sites, and more.

World Famous Comics

http://www.worldfamouscomics.com/news

Created by Justin Chung, World Famous Comics went on-line in 1995. The site, which is updated daily, offers users access to all kinds of articles about comics and graphic novels, including columns, reviews, news reports, and features, as well as a host of interactive resources.

Additional Periodical Articles with Abstracts

More information about graphic novels and comic books can be found in the following articles. Readers interested in additional articles may consult the *Readers' Guide to Periodical Literature* and other H.W. Wilson publications.

The Revolt of the Comic Books. Julian Sanchez. *American Prospect* v. 18 pp43–47 November 2007.

The post-September 11, 2001, era has seen an explosion of politically themed storylines in mainstream and independent comics, Sanchez reports. The illustrated universe's debate centers on preemptive war, warrantless surveillance, and the responsibility that comes with great power. Although not a new phenomenon, the politically inspired tales of the "war on terror" era have been remarkable for their ubiquity and sophistication and in the way they have laid bare, and sometimes exploded, the political ideas embedded in the superhero genre itself. The work of comics writers to grasp the current events raise the questions of whether the superhero is a natural neocon. For comics to succeed as modern political allegory, Sanchez writes, authors cannot simply transplant real controversies into their fictional worlds: they must invent a grammar and a vocabulary for a new type of superhero narrative.

Canadian Splendour. Jason McBride. *Canadian Business* v. 82 pp90–93 October 27–November 9, 2009.

Small Montreal-based firm Drawn & Quarterly (D&Q) has become a global player in the field of graphic novels, McBride writes. Founded in 1989 by Chris Oliveros, D&Q was the first North American publisher to consistently combine the sensibility and craftsmanship of art books and the high-mindedness of contemporary literature into the "literary graphic novel." Oliveros, who has now expanded into retailing with a store on Montreal's Bernard Street, plans to keep D&Q relatively small and focused.

The Not-So-Untold Story of the Great Comic-Book Scare. Gene Kannenberg, Jr. *The Chronicle of Higher Education* v. 54 ppB19–20 May 23, 2008.

Kannenberg reviews *The Ten-Cent Plague: The Great Comic-Book Scare and How It Changed America,* by David Hajdu. The most impressive aspect of Hajdu's book is the breadth of his primary research, including interviews with "more than 150 comic-book artists, writers, editors, publishers, readers, and others."

Alternative Cartoonists Nearing the Punch Line? Megan Tedy. *Extra!* v. 22 pp14–15 October 2009.

It took years for cartoonist Dan Perkins, aka Tom Tomorrow, to get his comic strip "This Modern World" syndicated in alternative weekly newspapers, but his career was knee-capped last January when Village Voice Media, publisher of 14 alternative weeklies, suspended all syndicated cartoons. Tedy discusses the difficulties facing a number of alternative publications that have traditionally been havens for alternative cartoonists.

Drawn-Out Sagas. Matthew Flamm. *Crain's New York Business* v. 20 pp3+ February 2–8, 2004.

In recent years, the graphic novel genre has been one of the few real success stories in the book publishing industry, where sales have been falling in virtually every category, Flamm observes. Two major book retailers, Borders and Barnes & Noble, have been rushing to add more shelf space for graphic novels, which were once the sole preserve of comic book stores.

Scholars See Comics as No Laughing Matter. Debra Viadero. *Education Week* v. 28 pp1+ February 11, 2009.

While some still view comics as "subliterature," Viadero reports, the medium is starting to gain acceptance among educators. In January 2009, Fordham University hosted "Graphica in Education," a first-of-its-kind symposium on teaching comics in the classroom, and in 2004, Maryland debuted its Comic Book Initiative, a program in which 80 schools around the state developed lesson plans involving graphic novels. While studies have yet to prove that comics make students better readers, research indicates they inspire young people to "read more, and read more varied types of literature," according to expert James "Bucky" Carter. Viadero also discusses the Comic Book Project, an after-school program that encourages students to write and draw their own comics.

Comics & Graphic Novels. Samantha Cleaver. *Instructer* v. 117 pp28–30+ May/June 2008.

The writer explores the potential of comics and graphic novels as tools for teaching reading. She describes a number of end-of-year activities based around comic books.

On Writing (And Reading) the Graphic Novel. Stefan Petrucha. *Knowledge Quest* v. 36 pp60–63 January/February 2008.

There are similarities and differences between graphic novels and prose, Petrucha observes. The basic goal of both is to convince the reader they are looking at something imaginatively alive. Prose is best at communicating a flow of thoughts but is less efficient when dealing with something like fast action. Meanwhile, graphic novel require readers to exercise both their verbal and visual imaginations simultaneously, creating a uniquely intimate experience that sits somewhere between film and prose.

What is Manga? Gilles Poitras. *Knowledge Quest* v. 36 p49 January/February 2008.

Manga, Japanese comic books published with every demographic and genre found in prose, fiction, and nonfiction, have seen stunning growth in the United States, Poitras reports. This growth can be attributed to the availability of manga for girls, a demographic that has been ignored in the U.S. comic industry; the availability of romance stories for boys; and the approachability of illustrated narratives for many readers who may be reluctant to pick up regular prose. Poitras discusses the differences between the visual structure of manga and traditional comic books.

More than Just Funny Books: Comics and Prose Literacy for Boys. Lessons in Learning. Canadian Council on Learning (on-line) July 21, 2010.

According to various studies of Canadian students, boys lag behind girls in terms of reading ability and enjoyment. With these findings in mind, the author of this article explains why comics are useful tools in encouraging boys to read. Research suggests males respond to visual media and prefer stories that incorporate elements of fantasy, horror, and adventure. Comics tend to satisfy both requirements, and according to the author, they have numerous educational benefits and often provide a "gateway" to traditional types of literature. Educators are also using comics to teach early readers, second-language learners, and children with learning disabilities, the author writes, suggesting the medium has finally broken free of its "low culture" stigma.

Drawn from Life. Brian Bethune. *Maclean's* v. 117 pp102–05 October 11–18, 2004.

Bethune reports that Canadian artists are leading the charge of graphic novels into the literary mainstream. According to Chris Oliveros, owner of Montreal-based Drawn & Quarterly (D&Q), which publishes most Canadian graphic novels, about half of the genre's stars are Canadians. Oliveros claims that Chester Brown's *Louis Riel*, published in 2003, was the latest groundbreaking work, which meant bookstores could sell comics to an older readership. Graphic novels that are maturely executed and themed and presented with D&Q's sumptuous production values are no longer dismissed just because they are comics.

After the Graphic Novel. Sid Jacobson. *The New Leader* v. 90 pp45–46 May/June–July/August 2007.

Jacobson believes that an ongoing process has steadily and radically transformed the art of cartoon continuity. Following the development of the newspaper comic strip and comic magazines, toward the end of the 20th century a change in distribution methods and the closing of comic book stores prompted a steep decline in magazine sales. Publishers reacted by developing titles for readers in their late teens and early 20s, while slowly abandoning those for younger readers. Another result of this dynamic was the emergence of a new form of the medium, dubbed the graphic novel. Now a growing number of publishers are keen to bring out graphic fiction, libraries and bookstores have established separate sections for it, and certain titles are earning literary awards. Given this new phenomenon, one option for future development could be graphic nonfiction. Jacobson also discusses *The 9/11 Commission Report,* a graphic nonfiction book that he worked on.

The Renegade Cartoonist: Enshrining Berkeley Breathed's 'Bloom County'. Brian Raftery. *New York* v. 42 pp94–96 October 19, 2009.

In 1989, Berkeley Breathed abandoned his Pulitzer Prize-winning comic strip, "Bloom County," at the peak of its popularity, just nine years after it was launched. To readers in 1980, Breathed's fusion of political satire, pop-culture, and interspecies existential crises expressed by a band of small-town eccentrics, human and otherwise, was anachronistic to the point of anarchy. In excerpts from their conversation, Raftery and Breathed discuss the latter's work.

Independent Spirit. Steven Heller. *Print* (New York, N.Y.) v. 59 p37 March/April 2005.

In this article, Heller presents a tribute to Will Eisner, pioneer of the graphic novel, who died on January 3, 2005, at the age of 87. Eisner's work *The Spirit*, launched in 1940 as a newspaper comics supplement, virtually invented the comic-book antihero and, by extension, the underground comic. He lived long enough to see the medium he pioneered, comics, and the genre he helped to define, the graphic novel, emerge from the margins of popular culture to become highly respected and commercially valued media.

The Young and the Graphic Novel. James Bickers. *Publishers Weekly* v. 254 pp62–63 February 19, 2007.

The landscape for graphic books for kids has changed considerably, Bickers observes. A market once dominated by manga has, over the past couple of years, witnessed the gradual entry of the graphic novel—typically a format used for adult titles. Most publishers attribute the changing face of the modern world as a prime mover behind the trend: Today's children are the first generation to grow up more used to digital screens than the printed page, and as wireless devices proliferate, kids increasingly understand and appreciate data that is sent to them in visual form. One of the most successful titles in this emerging space is Jeff Smith's *Bone*; originally published in comic-book form from 1991, *Bone's* 1,300-page epic journey is now being reissued in nine parts by Graphix, an imprint of Scholastic that focuses on graphic novels.

Comics Class of '08: Four New Graphic Novel Authors/Artists. Heidi MacDonald. *Publishers Weekly* v. 255 pp34, 36 May 5, 2008.

Talented young artists are making an impression in the comics world, MacDonald notes. The sudden upsurge in the success of graphic novels has greatly increased the opportunities available to young cartoonists. MacDonald goes on to explore the work of four such artists: Jeff Lemire, Dash Shaw, Hope Larson, and Eleanor Davis.

Jeff Smith on 'Bone.' Heidi MacDonald. *Publishers Weekly* v. 251 p34 October 18, 2004.

In a brief interview with MacDonald, cartoonist Jeff Smith, who recently wrapped up his 1300-page fantasy epic, *Bone,* after self-publishing it for 12 years, discusses the basic story of *Bone,* whether he would do more with the comic at a later stage, and his deal with Scholastic Books, which in January 2005 will begin reprinting the nine *Bone* volumes in full-color editions for the first time.

Françoise Mouly: Comics and Reading. Calvin Reid. *Publishers Weekly* v. 255 p27 December 8, 2008.

Françoise Mouly, *New Yorker* art director and wife and publishing collaborator of cartoonist Art Spiegelman, has had a huge influence on American reading culture, Reid reports. In 1980, as a young French student, Mouly teamed with Spiegelman to establish *RAW*, a lauded anthology series that highlighted experimentalist stories and graphics and had a strong influence on the alternative comics movement of the 1980s. In 2000, the couple launched Little Lit books at HarperCollins, basically a series of alternative comics for children. On her own, Mouly established Toon Books, a line of skillfully designed book-format comics for kids aged six and up, because she believes that comics have a unique pedagogical ability to foster the very act of reading in a child.

Comics Are Books, Too! Calvin Reid. *Publishers Weekly* v. 253 pp26–28+ March 20, 2006.

Illustrations of several contemporary American comic books are reproduced, alongside Reid's commentary, revealing the various shapes and sizes that these publications come in.

Art Spiegelman and Françoise Mouly: The Literature of Comics. Calvin Reid. *Publishers Weekly* v. 247 pp44–45 October 16, 2000.

According to Reid, Art Spiegelman, author of *Maus*, the Pulitzer Prize-winning Holocaust memoir-in-comics, and his wife, Françoise Mouly, art director of the *New Yorker*, are the first couple of provocative, sophisticated comics. The pair are founders of *RAW*, the trailblazing journal and publisher of alternative comics and cutting-edge graphics art. In addition, in October HarperCollins will issue Spiegelman and Mouly's *Little Lit: Folklore and Fairy Tale Funnies*, a large-format collection showcasing stories by comics artists and children's illustrators who offer an underground comics take on the children's picture book genre. *Little Lit*, the most recent in an ongoing publishing series by these two comics and graphic design veterans, is set apart by its offbeat storytelling and amazing graphics.

Janet Evanovich Mixes It Up. Sasha Watson. *Publishers Weekly* v. 257 p25 May 17, 2010.

In July, mother/daughter team Janet and Alex Evanovich will release the graphic novel *Troublemaker*, Watson reports. Fans will recognize the rambunctious, humorous, crime-tinged world of Alex Barnaby—and of Janet Evanovich more generally—but this is the first time that they will get to see it in full-color illustrations, with all the wild action splashed across the pages of a comic book.

American Born Chinese: Interview with G. Yang. Rick Margolis. *School Library Journal* v. 52 p41 September 2006.

Margolis conducts an interview with Gene Yang, author of *American Born Chinese*, a graphic novel that deals with racial prejudice. Yang talks about how he came up with the idea for this book, his own experiences of racism growing up, when he started to draw comics, how he developed his style of drawing, his day job, how Asian-Americans have reacted to *American Born Chinese*, and why one of the book's characters seems to be a caricature of all negative Chinese stereotypes combined.

Kids Love Comics, Too! Karen Bilton. *School Library Journal* v. 50 pp30–31 July 2004.

As comics and graphic novels gain acceptance as legitimate literature, teachers and librarians will need to consider which titles to include in their classrooms and libraries, Bilton observes. In this article, the author offers an overview of what comics and graphic novels librarians should add to their collections for grade-school-age children.

Nothing Comic About It. Van Jensen. *Sojourners* v. 38 pp 42–46 November 2009.

Over recent decades, comic books and graphic novels have started to address such issues as global politics, revolution, and religion in thoughtful and creative ways, Jensen observes. The comic industry has consequently mushroomed, particularly in the last five years, attracting ever increasing numbers of readers and bringing in substantial amounts of money, especially through film adaptations. Christian comics, however, have been appearing since the early 1940s, when the publisher M. C. Gaines created *Picture Stories From the Bible*, which initiated a long series of literal biblical translations, the most recent being R. Crumb's *The Book of Genesis*. Nevertheless, some believe that still more could be done in comics and graphic novels to accommodate cerebral readers. Within the industry, it is agreed that if the genre is to continue its current rate of growth and be taken seriously, its source material has to be nonfiction rather than fantasy.

Graphic Literacy. Keith McPherson. *Teacher Librarian* v. 33 pp67–69 April 2006.

The writer discusses the growing presence of graphic literature in school libraries and classrooms. This growth provides students, teachers, and teacher-librarians with new materials and opportunities to discover and develop engaging paths toward textual and visual literacy. McPherson also provides a number of resources for those wishing to initiate or expand a graphic literature collection.

Getting Students to Write Using Comics. Mark Crilley. *Teacher Librarian* v. 37 pp28–31 October 2009.

Crilley, author of the "Akiko" series of chapter books and the "Miki Falls" series of graphic novels, discusses his use of graphic novels to encourage students to write and enjoy it. He also explains three exercises he conducts when making presentations to schoolchildren.

Comic Belief. Meabh Ritchie. *The Times Educational Supplement* (on-line) December 11, 2009.

Exploring the educational benefits of producing—not just reading—graphic novels, Ritchie discusses *Fool's Gold*, a 132-page comic written and illustrated by students at England's Dearne High. Many Dearne students suffer from learning disabilities and come from low-income households, and as Ritchie reports, the project inspired participants in ways other assignments hadn't, leading some to consider careers in writing. In producing the book, students worked with published authors and delved into the history of Yorkshire, their home county. "They are taking pride in something that will be a memory for them all their lives," project coordinator Peter Shaw tells Ritchie.

What Is a Graphic Novel? Eddie Campbell. *World Literature Today* v. 81 p13 March/April 2007.

The term graphic novel is used in different ways, Campbell observes. It is used as a synonym for comic books. In addition, it is used to classify a format—for example, a bound book of comics—in contrast to the traditional stapled comic magazine. Graphic novel also refers to a comic book narrative that is equivalent in form and dimensions to the prose novel. Finally, some use the term to indicate a form that is more than a comic book in the scope of its ambition.

Index

About the Editor

KATHARINE "KAT" KAN has been reading comics for 50 years. She earned her B.A. (1977) and M.L.S. (1981) at the University of Hawaii-Manoa. She has worked as a children's and then young adult librarian for public libraries in Hawaii and Indiana, and she is now a part-time school librarian in the Florida Panhandle. She has been writing about graphic novels in libraries since 1994, mostly for *Voice of Youth Advocates,* and she reviews graphic novels, teen fiction, and adult mysteries for *VOYA* and for *Booklist.* She currently works as a Collection Development Librarian for Brodart's Books Division, and she is the selector for H.W. Wilson's *Graphic Novels Core Collection.*